Allison Romero's Prophecies

Allison Romero's Prophecies

Book One: "Lethal Rivalries"

Daisy Sepe

VANTAGE PRESS
New York

This is a work of fiction. Any similarities between the characters appearing herein and any real persons, living or dead, is purely coincidental.

Cover design by Susan Thomas

FIRST EDITION

All rights reserved, including the right of
reproduction in whole or in part in any form.

Copyright © 2004 by Daisy Sepe

Published by Vantage Press, Inc.
419 Park Ave. South, New York, NY 10016

Manufactured in the United States of America
ISBN: 0-533-14541-4

Library of Congress Catalog Card No.: 2003090636

0 9 8 7 6 5 4 3 2 1

Contents

One	Jenny, Ryan, and Allison	1
Two	The Eerie and the Haunting	8
Three	Dark Falls Junior High	13
Four	What Magic Could Do	23
Five	The Alibi	29
Six	Lazy Day	35
Seven	The Feigned Sleep-Over	37
Eight	Witches' Night Out	44
Nine	Allison Romero: Witch's Apprentice	52
Ten	Our Gigantic Problem	57
Eleven	The Risk	66
Twelve	A More Than Queer Morning	73
Thirteen	Regretful	85
Fourteen	Gym-Nausea	94
Fifteen	The Stick and the Stone	98
Sixteen	The Mandate of Hecate	105
Seventeen	Vision in the Water	115
Eighteen	A Beginning to Doom	121
Nineteen	The Reverie Potion	124
Twenty	The Nightmare	129
Twenty-one	The Enemy	134
Twenty-two	A Day to Remember	143

AND SO ON...   155

Allison Romero's Prophecies

One
Jenny, Ryan, and Allison

Allison Romero peered from behind a bush, where she had been crouching in silence, afraid of being spotted.

"Give it up, *Ryan!*" taunted a girl who, she discovered, went by the name Jenny. She was a tan Chinese girl, about five feet tall, and was smiling, evilly. "You and your weakling coven don't stand a *chance* against *my powerful one!*"

"I'd never . . . surrender . . . to . . . you . . . good for nothing . . . **SNOBS!**" panted Ryan, a tall, light-skinned Asian boy with a slightly feminine face. He was tied to a wooden post. After saying this, the evil smile on Jenny's face darkened.

"I wouldn't have said that if I were you," said Jenny in a calm voice, motioning her index finger from left to right, a grin that showed hunger for vengeance added to the darkness of her face. She lit a black candle, holding it with her right hand. On the ground, was an old worn-out book with a leather cover. She bent down, and with her free hand, carelessly thumbed through the fragile, old parchment pages. When she picked it up, she cast another hungry grin at Ryan.

"No!" whispered Ryan, his eyes widening.

Jenny's smile became yet icier. She started reading

from the book, "Ascendis, ascendis! Bring to me the soul of my utmost enemies!"

"No!"

"May he slash and bleed, that no sore will go nor heed!"

"No!"

"Burn his flesh and eat his voice, may he suffer, without any choice!"

"**NOOO!**"

A blinding flash shot out from the blackish-blue sky. It sped towards Ryan. Allison didn't know what came over her, but despite her fear, she popped out from her hiding place. With fiery eyes, she ran towards Jenny.

"Castiramius reverio!" she bellowed, holding a crystal-blue bottle, which was shaped as an overturned teardrop with a smooth bottom. Jenny turned to her in shock. Allison and Jenny had their eyes fixed on each other. Everything seemed to be in slow motion. Right in front of her was Jenny, her target, and to the right, was helpless Ryan, ready to get struck by the possibly deadly, rapidly traveling beam in the sky.

What should she do? Should she strike her target before it could escape, or risk it all to rescue the boy—who had just fainted—from a wretched death? Her mind was racing—she couldn't think—she was so panicked—all she felt like doing was screaming. . . .

"Allison! Allison!" a calm and gentle voice was calling her.

"*Errrrr.* . . . **I CAN'T TAKE IT ANYMORE!**" she shrieked loudly.

There was a pause. "Can't take *what, anak?*" asked the soothing voice.

Allison opened her eyes, and stared around. Soon, she realized that she was in her bedroom. *It was only a dream!* A very queer one too! How could that be? It all seemed so *real*. The night air, the energy . . . the fear . . . she felt them all.

She looked up and right above her was her mother. "Can't take *what, anak?*" she repeated. (*Anak* means *child* in the Filpipino language.)

"Oh, n–nothing, just a dream I had," she replied, although she had this intense gut feeling that it was more than *just* a dream.

"Well, all right then. Come down to breakfast, okay? We'll be leaving soon." Allison's mother turned to leave, but as if she had just remembered something, turned back. "Oh, and by the way, happy birthday!" She kissed Allison on the forehead and walked out, shutting the door behind her.

Allison and her parents were moving away from their home in Los Angeles, California, to this "nowhere place" (as Allison called it) called Dark Falls. She didn't even know where Dark Falls was located.

Is there something else? Oh yes, this day, May 13, 2001, was her thirteenth birthday. Sometimes, she could go anywhere unperceived on her own birthday. She could even go to her own birthday party, stand under a festive banner with her name colorfully printed on it, and the guests would probably ask in a puzzled way, something more or less like this, "*Whose* birthday is it today?" That is, if she ever had one. Never in her thirteen years has she had even one family birthday dinner.

There's something else, eerie to the extent of horrifying, about Allison Romero's birth date. She was born on May 13, 1988; a Friday. Someone very superstitious would think a person who was born on a Friday the thirteenth was cursed or something. . . .

When her mother's footsteps died away, she sat up,

and thought about the dream. It made no sense to her whatsoever. Who're Ryan and Jenny? Why did she have this bizarre dream? What were those words she was yelling? What in the world is a coven? These questions raced through her mind.

"*Ally-son!*" shouted her mom. In an instant, the girl popped up, took off her blue pajamas, flung on a shirt, and pulled on some jeans. After this, she rushed out of her room, went down the hallway, and—*wait!* Pause everything!

Do you see that girl who just ran of her room? The one who's getting ready to run down those stairs? Of course not, this is a book! Besides, I didn't describe her yet.

Allow me to start by introducing her. Her name is Allison Romero. Yes, a typical thirteen-year-old girl she was, until she moved to her new home in Dark Falls. She had dark brown hair that was always in a simple ponytail. Saying she's Filipina (Female term for *Filipino*) isn't essential enough. Let's see, she has tan skin, is a bit short for her age, and has brown eyes, which had a mixture of ethnic background. Like most Filipino people, her eyes were bewildering. You couldn't tell what her ethnicity was. Let's just say that they were Mexican-but-not-really-sort-of-kind-of-Asian eyes.

On her left shoulder, she had an odd birthmark, which was the shape of a serpent. It wasn't a perfect-looking snake, but it was clear to see that it was not an ordinarily shaped birthmark. She would always insist that it meant something, though her parents would assure her that she was mistaken.

She also liked to do most things in a rush, as you might have noticed already ... well, actually, I don't know why she's in a rush, but I guess that's because she's excited *(yeah, right!)*. Here is a short list of other information on Allison Romero:

Is a female
Favors spiders
Enjoys Italian and Filipino foods
Was born in Los Angeles, California
Likes every shade of blue
Enjoys nature
Cherishes friends
Has Pinay (Filipina) pride
Loves to read novels
Cannot draw
Doesn't know what a coven is
Just had a weird dream
Is who this story's about
Was in her former middle school's drill team
Is Jay-Ar and April Romero's daughter
Likes to play Scrabble and Chess
Doesn't like to do research
Likes shiny objects: glass, crystal, glossy water, etc.
Prefers cats (black), if not spiders
Is a "clever" spy gadget inventor
Loves surprises
and
Is not a
super-kid-like-main-child-characters-usually-are-in-novels, but a typical-ordinary-kid-like-in-reality

There's just one thing I haven't included yet. I just know it was the most important thing of all. What was it, what was it? I *know,* Allison Romero is, of course, me!

Now, where was I? Ah, yes, *I* sped out of *my* room, went down the hallway, and sprinted down the stairs. I ran into the kitchen, and there was my mom, sipping a mug of coffee. She's going to take another sip . . . pause it. Okay, that's my mom, April Romero. Well, she used to be my dad's partner in his chemistry work. Now, she's a housewife. I know, *boring.* All right, let's get back to the story now.

I sat on the chair across from her.

"There you a—" she started, but stopped and watched me as I devoured my pancakes and gulped down my orange juice in bewilderment.

As soon as I finished, I zoomed back up to my room, grabbed my bags, raced down the stairs, and opened the front door, staring down at the driveway. My dad was already loading up the red mini van. He's lifting a box into the van. . . . *pause.*

Yeah, that's my dad, Jay-Ar Romero. He looks about the same as me. Our eyes, our skin, they're identical! Well, he, you know, doesn't have the feminine features of me, though! As you know, he's a chemist. That's why we had to move. He got a new job at that nowhere place. Now, again, back to the story.

My backpack straps were cutting my shoulders, and my duffel bags felt like they weighed a ton, so I placed them into the van.

"Hey, kiddo!" called my dad. "Happy B-day!"

I smiled. "Hi, Dad! No presents?"

"Well, gee, I thought you knew that our new house would be your gift."

I knew that this was an excuse for not buying me a gift, but I gladly replied, "Oh, yeah! I forgot!" With another smile, I said, "I'll just wait in the van." As I sat on the comfortable back seat of the vehicle, I thought deeply of the dream. In about thirty minutes, my parents were both ready, and we all set off, saying bye forever to Los

Angeles, to California, and hello to our new home, which was awaiting our arrival in the unpopular town called Dark Falls.

Two
The Eerie and the Haunting

Once our house was out of sight, I faced forward, thinking about the dream again. It certainly was out of the ordinary. I never once in my life heard of a coven, nor had I seen the faces of those two teens before. I was hearing—and if I wasn't mistaken—*saying* some of the most far out, alien, weird, freaky, supernatural, psychopathic, peculiar, quirky, whatever-you-want-to-describe-odd-as words. It was like something you would read about in make-believe books. All dreams are odd, I knew, but this dream made me feel as if it were more than just a crazy trick of the sandman, but why? Maybe it was because that, unlike most dreams, I wasn't in one place at first then turning around to find myself somewhere else completely, or anything. It made sense, yet didn't.

After about an hour, we came to a stop. My mind came out of reverie, and we went out. We were at a rest stop. It was desolate, except for two box-shaped restrooms, which were made of logs, and a few splintered tables stood in an untidy manner.

A sudden breeze brushed through my hair, and a tumbleweed the size of a soccer ball bounced by me. It was very, very silent. Not the serene kind of silent, but the bone-chilling kind. I got goose bumps watching the eerie sight. This made me shudder all over.

At that moment, my parents approached me. "I think we should go," said my mom. "The restrooms are locked." I didn't have to go anyway. We all sat in the van again.

As we drove, I gazed out the window. There was nothing but vast land, covered with tall golden-brown grass and tumbleweeds. My spine began to tingle looking at such loneliness. Not one living thing but us was to be seen.

Though it was only one 'o clock in the afternoon, the atmosphere became much darker. Soon, we came across a sign that had words painted in red, somewhere in the woods.

WELCOME TO DARK FALLS

The soothing sound of pouring water started to break the silence, and foliage of many hues lay sprinkled everywhere as if it were autumn. We drove through a narrow, rugged dirt path, which was called Dark Lane, and up a rocky driveway. We were at our new home, 2085 Scare Realm Avenue. It was a large, two-story, cabin-like house. There were only a few neighboring houses, and the entire area seemed to be made up of woods. Trees walled the view in every direction. The sound of pouring, splashing water broke through the utter silence.

I wanted to venture through the woods, so I went up to my parents. "Mom, could I—"

"Sure," she replied before I could finish my question, "just come home before it gets any darker, okay?"

I nodded, then ran off, searching for something of interest. Soon I was at the edge of the wood, and the place was clear of trees. I heard the sound of splashing water. Right ahead of me, was a small waterfall and a glassy stream that was a yard wide. It stretched endlessly into the woods, the trees parting like people making way for a queen's red carpet. There were fish beneath the clear, glistening water. Full of wonder, I attempted to stick my hand in.

"I wouldn't do that if I were you," warned an expressionless voice behind me. I jumped, startled. "I'm sorry for scaring you, it's just that those fish are carnivorous."

The person talking to me, was a tall, light-skinned, Asian boy—Chinese, I thought—with a slightly girlish face. He was wearing a black trench coat, which went down to his knees, a black turtleneck, and a pair of black slacks. Black, highly polished dress shoes concealed his feet. His black hair was neatly parted on the side by a strictly straight line. My jaws dropped, because I knew at once that it was . . .

"My name is Ryan," he greeted, sticking out his hand.

"Allison. My name is Allison," I said, shaking his hand as I stared into his dark-brown eyes, awestricken.

"New here?" he asked.

"Er, what? Oh, yes. Got here just now," I replied, coming out of my thoughts. "Just thought I'd look around and . . ." I stopped, seeing that he continued to stare at me, motionless and expressionless.

"Do you believe in witches?" he asked finally.

"Well, I, erm—"

"If you don't, I suggest you start believing now," he interrupted. All of a sudden, unearthly howls of wolves stirred through the darkening atmosphere. He looked up and around. "Well, it's getting dark, you should head for home." He walked through the thick underbrush, disappearing into the trees. I was so positive that there were no houses there, so why would he go there?

My thoughts trailed off on my way home. All I thought about was the Ryan in my dream, and the expressionless Ryan whom I just met. Could they be the same person? How could I have a dream pertaining to people I have never even seen in my whole life? I started believing that my dream really had a meaning, but what?

"*Aiy, Dios Ko, anak!*" (Oh my God, child!) "Where have you been? You scared me! Why are you back so late?!" scolded my mom. I was already at the front door of 2085 Scare Realm Avenue. "It's very dark out!"

"I—" before I could explain, she just told me to go to bed.

She led me through the house. Though undecorated, it looked beautiful. She led me through a warm living room, into the cozy family room, and down a hallway. To the sides, were the master bedroom, a small windowless room, and a large kitchen. After passing the kitchen, we went into the dining room, which was two times larger than the large kitchen. We turned right, went through an arched entryway, and went up a flight of white carpeted steps. When we reached the top, I saw a rather long hallway to the left. To the right, a tall painting of a vase hung. "Your room is on the last door on the left side of the hall," directed my mom. "I put all your belongings inside, and there's a sleeping bag and a pillow on the floor."

She walked back down the stairs. I walked to the last door to the left. When I entered, I shut the door and walked inward. I stood still in the center of the dimly lit room.

Ah-ooo! Aw aw-ooooo! Haunting howls of wolves filled the room. It made the hairs on the back of my neck shoot up. The calm and steady wind began to screech and moan, making my heart pound faster and faster. I started to look around through wide eyes, breathing with much difficulty . . .

Swish! A gust of icy wind filtered into the room. The

window had been flung open by the powerful wind. I calmly walked towards it, relieved that it wasn't *somebody* who opened it. When I had closed it, I quickly changed into my pajamas, shut the lights, wrapped myself in the sleeping bag, and shortly dozed off. I didn't care if I slept too early. The day wasn't full of events, but I was sure tired. Anyway, I was looking forward to a new day at my new school.

Three
Dark Falls Junior High

"Rise and shine, sleepy head!" exclaimed my dad cheerfully. "It's time to go to school."

"Wha' time is i'?" I groaned into my pillow.

"Seven in the morning!" he answered. I popped up. "I'll see you at breakfast!" He walked out of the room. I wriggled my way out of the sleeping bag.

After grabbing a towel, I searched for the bathroom. I searched all around the house, then felt idiotic discovering that the bathroom was a door down from my bedroom. After finding it, I took a quick—though refreshing—shower. Soon after, I was dressed in my new flare jeans, and my new sky-blue, three quarter-sleeved shirt. Before going down to breakfast, I tied my hair in the usual ponytail.

I walked down the stairs, and followed the delectable aroma of scrambled eggs and coffee. After arriving at the kitchen, I gobbled down some buttered toast and scrambled eggs. At the same time, I freely helped myself to some O.J. once the pitcher was set on the table.

I then grabbed my bag and ran to the front door. Before I could touch the door knob, my dad came up to me. He was jingling the keys to the van. "Are you sure you don't want *me* to drop you off at school?"

I opened the door. "No, I'm sure I can manage." I

walked out the door and down the driveway. After taking a right turn, I felt something was wrong with my route.

"Need help finding your way?" I heard Ryan's monotonous voice. "School's that way." He was pointing to the left (opposite of where I was going). His clothes looked the same, except for his turtleneck, which was a stretchy gray one. Not a single strand of hair interfered with his girlish face.

"Oh! I—er—just looking for my—my ring!" I lied, turning slightly pink. "Oh! Here it is!" I bent down, and clutched my hand, pretending to pick up a ring.

"*Right,* and I'm a girl!" he joked, although still very expressionless. "Here, just follow me. Oh. yeah, here's your program slip."

He handed me a piece of paper containing my class information. It told me the names of my teachers for each class, which period I had them, and my classroom numbers.

"You and I have P.E. and homeroom together," he pointed out. "Your elective's painting, huh? It's mine too."

I didn't know what to say. "Oh . . . okay. Um, how did you get this?"

"Principal gave it," he replied quickly.

"How did you know where I lived? Why did she or he let *you* give it to me?"

"Mister Kaehler—that's the principal, Jamal Kaehler—mailed it to me. Can we get to school now? We might get a tardy. Not good for your first day."

"Well, okay," I replied passively.

On our way to school, he made steps so gigantic for me that I had to jog to catch up. We kept silent most of the way. As we walked through the woods, the foliage began to sprinkle down on us, and the peaceful sound of the waterfall never sounded better! It felt like too perfect a day to spend at school.

Soon the spongy moss-carpeted earth was replaced by rough asphalt. I figured out that we had reached the school grounds. All around me, were weary looking teens who were all wearing black or gray. They eyed me with their shadowed eyes. Many of them were pale and lean.

I continued to walk towards the school building, trying to ignore their dead stares. They felt impossible to ignore though, even through a turned back. When I reached the front double-doors of the giant building, I saw a huge marble sign above the doorway. I gazed at it for a moment. In red letters, it said: Dark Falls Junior High School.

"Allison, I presume?" asked a voice of a girl, which was as dull as Ryan's. I looked to the side, to find that Ryan wasn't by me anymore.

"Yes, she *must* be!" gushed the subtly more lively voice of another girl. "I mean, look at her, all cheery and all."

I turned around. There standing in amazement, was a tall, slim, Cambodian girl with a swarthy complexion. She wore a dark gray, three-quarter-sleeved turtleneck, and slim flared pants, which were black. Right beside her, was a tall Chinese girl, who was three shades lighter than me. She was fiddling around with a round, palm-sized amethyst. A black cloak was wrapped around her.

"Well, are you?" she asked again.

"Uh, wha'—oh, yeah. Yes I am," I was busy studying their features, to see if I'd seen them before, "and you are . . . ?"

"Phanny!" gushed the skinny Cambodian girl, happily, though she didn't look it. "That's *Paw-nee.*"

"My name is Karen." She didn't sound as joyous as Phanny.

"Nice to meet you!" I replied smiling. My smile quickly faded, seeing that neither of them had the slightest grin. "So . . . how did you know my name?" They continued giving me their dull stares.

"I told Ryan she wouldn't be fit for a witch," mumbled Karen through the corner of her mouth.

"She isn't one of us." Ryan had just appeared from nowhere. "I thought I had made it clear last night. Besides, we'll be able to make her a witch."

"Where *were* you? One of *who*?" I asked, but he went on.

"That would give us the opportunity to add to our coven. *And* we'll out number *Jenny's* coven!"

Ryan was now smiling radiantly, his eyes glistening with determination. It was the first time I'd seen him make any sort of facial expression.

"But what about Tay Song?" asked Phanny, sounding worried.

"Her? Oh she's only a fantastic acrobat, but she doesn't know anything about witchcraft. Allison will, though. We'll be four, while Jenny—who only has that Katrina Santiago and Krystine Mendoza as witch companions—will be one of three."

"Ha! Adding *her* into the coven wouldn't make a slight difference!" Karen laughed sarcastically.

"Um, what's all this talk about being a *witch* and being in your *coven?*" I asked, puzzled. "And who's Tay Song?"

Karen was about to say something full of discrimination, but Ryan gave her a gesture to stop. He drew a long sigh.

"She's an acrobat from school," informed Phanny.

"Hangs around with *Jenny* and her coven. You'll see them at P.E. Oh, right you don't know them." She sneered when saying "Jenny."

I just remembered that *Jenny* was in that dream I had, and so was Ryan. Instead of telling them this, I decided to do it later.

Ryan shot a frown at Phanny.

"*What!*" exclaimed Phanny.

"She was asking *me.*"

"*Oh, well sorry!*" said Phanny, sarcastically.

He rolled his eyes, then started explaining everything to me. "We are witches. Most of the inhabitants of Dark Falls are. That's kind of the reason why everyone here favors the color black, but not really. Now, a coven is a group of witches. Usually, the covens of Dark Falls come out to the woods around midnight to do their witchcraft. That's why you see all the students tired and shadow-eyed, and that's why I went among the trees the other night, to do witchcraft with the coven." He jerked his head towards Karen and Phanny.

"Now, I *know* what you're thinking. We don't have green faces and flying broomsticks, so how are we considered witches? Simple, we do witchcraft. All that other stuff are stereotypes. We're not in a Harry Potter book, you know."

"Oh, so you're *all* witches?"

"All three of us. Well, I'm a warlock. I *am* a boy."

"Uh huh . . . right. Question, do covens get named?"

"Depends if the leader wants to name it."

"Who's the leader of *your* coven?"

"Me, of course!" he said in a conceited way.

"So, tell me, what did *you* name your coven?"

Ryan gave an uneasy sigh. "*Ryan's kizz ony conin,*" he mumbled, turning pink.

"I'm sorry, could you repeat that?"

"Ryan's ki only cummin."

"Come again?"

"RYAN'S KIDS ONLY COVEN!" he boomed, furiously turning red.

I snorted, then chuckled, and I suddenly burst into out-of-control laughter. "HA, HA, HA! I'm so sorry, it's just, HA! Kids only! Ryan's, ha, ha, ha, ha! What a name for a, ha, teen-hage, teenage coven!" I continued to chortle.

"I know it's out of our age group," said Ryan, shuffling his feet, his head hung down. "The three of us started doing witchcraft amazingly early. I guess we were about five when we started this coven. Of course, we were planning to officially change the name."

"What about *Ryan's coven?*" I suggested.

"Nah, too plain."

Bong! Bong! Bong! Bong! The deafening sound of a bell felt as if it were vibrating inside of me.

"What's that?" I shouted, trying to muffle the noise by clasping my hands to my ears.

"It's called a *school bell,*" informed Karen, giving me a *where-in-the-universe-did-you-come-from* look. "It means school's about to start."

"Sound's more like the bell from the *Hunchback of Notre Dame,*" I muttered.

"Can we go inside now?" interrupted Phanny.

They led me inside the building. We turned left and went down a long hallway. When we got to the door that had a gilded number 115 metal plate on it, we entered.

"Welcome to homeroom," notified Phanny, now talking in a dull voice. She shut the door behind her and the three took their seats, leaving me standing at the front of the classroom.

When the *Bong! Bong! Bong! Bong!*ing of the bell rang again, the door flung open. A plump woman wearing a black dress that touched the floor stood in the doorway. She wore black lipstick, black eyeliner, and black eyeshadow.

"Good morning, students," she greeted. Her voice sounded sluggish and mournful, and she had a French accent. She scanned the room with her eyes, then landed on me. "We 'ave a new student joining aus today. May I eentroduce Mees Allyson Romero."

Everyone just continued to give me their dead stares. She let out a false cough.

"My name ees Madame Savant." She gave me a firm handshake.

Her eyes were scanning the room again. Apparently, she was looking for a vacant seat, because her eyes stopped at every seat of an absent student. She would say things like '. . . no zat's Nicole's seat' or '. . . zat's an absentee's seat'. There was hardly an unassigned seat anywhere.

"Ah," she said finally, "please occupy zee seat between Meester Nakano, and Meess Soi. Um, vaise your hands please." Phanny and Ryan raised their hands lazily, not bothering to raise them above their heads. "Zere, you shall seet."

When the unbearably loud bell rang fifteen minutes later, everyone stood up (oddly in unison), and grabbed their books and bags. Out in the halls, there were students flowing out from all directions. As we walked, Ryan and Karen headed a different way, leaving Phanny and me to room 207.

Mister Cross, our math teacher, was a ghost-white, slim, and tall man, who wore black pants and a tailcoat. His jet-black hair was slicked back, and on his face was a thin curled mustache. His voice was deep, and had a touch of an aristocratic accent.

"You will sit next to Howie Blanks." He assigned me a seat next to a thin and pale boy, whose cheekbones were very visible. He never blinked at all, so his gray eyes were always visible. As Mister Cross wrote problems on the blackboard, it made a piercing, screeching noise that gave me goose bumps. The others, however, just continued to copy down the problems into their notebooks as if there wasn't a single sound.

The day passed so gradually. In room 309, Mister Boris, our one-eyed, hunched-back history/geography teacher, talked in a high, creepy, scratchy voice, which gave me chills. His eyepatch had a black-and-white spiral design that got me woozy.

Miss Nightingale, our English teacher of room 502, was a woman who had the image of what I imagined a nymph must look like (delicately petite, slender, light-skinned, blue-eyed, and blonde), except for the fact that her dress was black, and her face lacked the nymph-like cheeriness. She talked in a distant voice, which was soft and ghostly. Her voice made me drowsy, but had no effect on others at all.

Ryan and I met in the art building for fourth period. Our painting teacher, Mister Bonaventura, was a short, skinny man, who wore a gray beard, dark sunglasses, a French beret, a tight pair of black pants, and a tight black turtleneck. He was somewhat like a hippy, talking in "psychedelic" slang, and wearing a large pendant of the "peace" symbol. He made us paint what he called "groovy swirls," which were merely multicolored swirls on a canvas. Ha, ha, ha . . . he was so high!

"Ya gotta get your brush on the right groove." His voice blended into the background in painting class. "The swirls've got to have righteous coloration, man! That black painting's gonna bring bad karma! You've got the groove, cool cat! Oh, that's the bell! See ya'll on the flip-side!"

My science teacher, Mr. Shnrub, was a Jamaican man who sounded as if he were talking into a kazoo. It took all my concentration to resist laughter, so I didn't concentrate on my work. Lucky for me, I didn't have homework for any of those classes.

P.E. was the class I was most active in. Miss Felton, a Brit, was a pretty tough physical education teacher for a scrawny-looking woman. She was pale, and wore the gym uniform: black fleece shorts and a gray T-shirt. We observed her doing back flips and somersaults on the gym mats. I was stunned by her agility and outstanding reflexes.

We each got a turn to test our skills. The first to go was the light-skinned Cambodian girl named Tay Song. She didn't look like much of an acrobat to me, but surely I was wrong. For a tiny girl, she was amazing, because she was as agile and as exciting to watch as the teacher herself. As we went down the list, each person's skills were more exemplary than the other.

After Ryan did his breathtaking performance, I heard something that made me forget about the amazing moves that each student made.

"Jenny Tsan!" called Miss Felton in her tough voice. There, walking towards the center of the giant mat, was the lightly tanned Chinese girl from the dream! The girl Ryan and them were talking about was the same one from the dream. Ryan was also in the dream. Was it possible that my dream was somewhat like a prophecy that I would have to fulfill in the near future . . . ?

"Miss Romero! Miss Romero!" I heard Miss Felton's

tough voice calling me. I was so busy thinking about the dream and the girl, that I forgot where I was. "Miss Romero, you're up."

"Huh?" I could feel the stares stab me from all over.

"It's your turn." She looked at me, confused.

"Oh!" I felt my face rapidly turning red. "I'm so sorry, Miss Felton."

"Are you all right?" she asked, very concerned.

"Yes," I said dryly.

I walked towards the center, full of humiliation. Lucky for me, I was in the school drill team for two years, the second year being the previous year. That meant a few simple flips would be no problem, but it didn't hold a candle to everyone else's abilities. It was fine. All I had to do, were the parts of my routine that pertained to the flipping, jumping, and cartwheels. My peers were pleased, seeing that the "newcomer" had any ability to do these things at all, and so was the teacher.

Four
What Magic Could Do

The sound of the deafening bell banged against my eardrums again. Everyone marched into the locker rooms (the boys and girls into separate rooms, of course). In about ten minutes, Karen, Ryan, Phanny, and I were together in the halls. School was over at last!

Ryan was walking near the wall, where he and Howie Blanks accidentally bumped into each other.

"Oh, no!" shrieked Howie, terrified. "I'm so very sorry, Ryan! I—I didn't mean to do that. I'll do anything to make it up to you. Here, I'll shine your shoes."

"No, it's o—"

"Oh, I know they're already polished!"

"It's okay, How—"

"I'll give you all my money, h—how's that?"

"It's not—"

"I'll do whatever you want, just don't curse me!"

"**HOWIE!**" boomed Ryan. Howie stopped dead. Ryan deeply inhaled, then spoke, "It's all right. I'm okay, and you're okay. Besides, it was an accident."

"You, you mean you *won't* curse me?"

Ryan swayed his head. "You *know* I would never use magic to hurt the innocent. Now go where you were heading."

Howie ran when hearing these words.

"What's up with him?" I asked Ryan, who watched Howie bump into other people as he frantically dashed through the hallway.

"His family and relatives died from a serious death-curse dilemma," he answered, still watching Howie.

"Move out of the way, *Ryanna!*" yelled a passerby, shoving Ryan.

"Let's go outside and discuss this," mumbled Ryan through the corner of his mouth. We walked through the main door, and out into the free world. Ryan led us to the edge of the woods. "This curse, like all death curses, was evil, but it was the most dire known to all sorcerers, witches, and warlocks. It was so powerful, that every single one of Howie's relatives were affected by it. Its original name was *Ultimus Vindicta,* but after the first time of its use after hundreds of years, this forgotten curse was renamed, *The Heinous Curse of '98.*"

"But why wasn't *he* killed?" I asked in an unnecessary whisper.

"The death of his entire relations was all it took to make him suffer, at least, that's my theory. Now, he lives with foster parents, who are said to hate his guts."

"It seems that that *was* his curse," I added, "to be orphaned at . . . *2001* . . . *minus 1998* . . . um . . . *at the age of ten.*"

"Yeah," agreed Ryan. "That curse is what made him turn away from witchcraft for good. He's too scared to do anything with it. That's why he got terrified when we bumped into each other. He thought that we'd curse him or something. It's weird how he got scared of *me.*" He lowered his head.

I knew what was coming. "*Oh, don't say that,*" I said comfortingly. "*I don't think you're pathetic.*"

He shot up and flushed. "*What?* No, no. I didn't mean that! I meant to say that he was a member of this coven!"

"He was?"

"Yeah."

"*Oh,*" I said, turning red. He stared forward for a moment.

"You sit next to him in math class, don't you, Allison?" Phanny had broken this embarrassing scene.

"Yeah, it's creepy how he doesn't blink."

"He's been like that since the curse. People say he cries all night and doesn't sleep, so his eyes are permanently open. I don't think it's true, though. I think it was part of the curse."

"We've got to go," whispered Ryan. "Follow me."

A peek of sunlight penetrated through the thick layer of greenery as we walked through the woods. The air was crisp and cool. Sprinkling foliage brightened the dull and plain colors of the woods. As I inhaled the refreshingly cool air, I felt like dancing and singing as the beautifully colored leaves showered on me. It was such a lovely afternoon, and knowing that I didn't have homework made me skip around, *literally.*

"What're you doing?" asked Phanny. She, Karen, and Ryan were looking at me as if I were in a quiet library, wearing an ape suit and prancing around through the aisles like an idiot.

"Oh, I was just, uh . . ." My face became scarlet, and I felt nine times smaller.

"Let me guess, you're *intrigued* by the colorful foliage, and no homework means you're free the entire evening, right?" guessed Phanny. Everyone was smiling now. Wow, after knowing them as dull and joyless teens for a whole day, I thought they would never smile. They were waiting for me to reply.

"Uh, *yes,*" a feeble voice came out of my mouth.

Their smiles cracked into hordes of cackles.

"You're—you're kidding, right?" panted Karen.

"What's so funny?!" I demanded, irritated. "Are you trying to peeve me for pleasure?"

"Do people from California dance around when they see something as common as colorful falling leaves?" grinned Phanny.

"N—no. And, what do you mean by *'people from California?'* This is still California, isn't it? I mean, it only took about *two hours* to get here!"

"I've never met such a weird person!" she went on, as if she didn't hear me. "And, girl, your evening *will* be free, from now till seven, anyway. You're coming with—"

"Phanny!" Ryan stopped her. "Not here!"

"Oh, right, sorry!"

"Phanny," called Karen.

"What?"

"Say it, but don't spray it, okay!"

Phanny noticed she had some saliva dangling from the corner of her mouth. She then noticed that she had been spitting at us as she talked. The other two stared at her.

All of a sudden, I remembered about the dream and Jenny.

That's when I realized that I had never told Ryan about him being in it yet.

"You guys," I called. Phanny was dawned out from the center of attention, "I want to ask you some questions, if you wouldn't mind."

"*Yeah?*" they all said together in an *I'm listening* sort of way.

"You know that girl named Jenny." They all winced at the instant I mentioned the name.

"Enemy!" shouted Ryan. "She's our ultimate rival! Her and her good-for-nothing *'Three L. W.'* coven."

"Three L. W.?" I asked.

"Yeah," said Ryan. "It's her coven's name. It stands for *'Three Lil' Witches.'* "

"Why are you asking us about her, *anyway?*" demanded Karen, suddenly being suspicious. "Are you being paid to be their *spy*? Getting information from us, *hmmm?*"

Ryan came up and reminded her vigorously, "Now, Karen, she just moved here. She couldn't have met Jenny and made a paying deal all in one day!"

"How do *you* know? She could be a witch who's pretending to be an ordinary girl."

"For goodness sakes, Karen, she's so clueless on everything we say about witchcraft. And also, I thought you were the most *practical* among the three of us, but now, I'm on the verge of kicking your—"

"Hey! Hey!" yelled Phanny quickly, obviously not wanting him to say the last word. "Shut it, and let Allison talk!" They both hushed in an instant, and faced me, attentively.

"No, I'm not their *spy,* but well, she was in a dream I—" I was suddenly interrupted.

"Hey **Ryanna!**" Jenny Tsan, Tay Song, Katrina Santiago, and Krystine Mendoza emerged from the thick wall of trees and shrubs. "Fonny and Amethyst Girl trying to give you a makeover?!" The other girls sniggered. "Hopefully that's so, 'cause you *really* need one!"

"Oh, shut your big fat mouth!" yelled Phanny. "And it's *Paw-nee,* not *Fonny!*"

"My mouth is a fairly normal size, unlike yours, *Fonny!*" said Jenny, haughtily. "Did the doctors *seriously* allow you to have an amino collagen shot? It's a wonder why they couldn't tell that your lip was already too fat!"

"*Shut up!* Yours will be even bigger—when my fist *accidentally* collides into your face!"

"I'd like to see you try!"

"All right I will!"

"Bring it on!"

Phanny was ready to charge, with her fists upheld, and her eyes—which seemed to be blazing—were fixed on Jenny. Tay leapt into the air, and did a somersault, landing an inch away from Phanny's face. Jenny just continued to smile her vain smile, her arms crossed.

Suddenly, Karen went in between them, and broke the fight-to-be by firmly saying, "Can't we just settle this some *other* time?"

"But—" Phanny was ready to object, but Karen shot a look of disapproval at her. She drew out some breath and slowly lowered her fists, full of disappointment.

"Fine, I wouldn't want to break a nail fighting someone who isn't *worth* winning over, anyway!" sneered Jenny.

"Oh, that's it! You're goin' down, Tsan!!!—" Phanny growled, ready to fight, but Karen and Ryan both clutched her shoulders tightly, afraid that she might spring onto Jenny and fight.

"Come on," whispered Karen vigorously, "it's not worth getting knocked out! Let's go!"

Phanny gave one last glare at Jenny, and followed us into the woods. Phanny grumbled, "*You wouldn't be so tough if your somersaulting bodyguard wasn't there to defend you!*"

Five
The Alibi

After about five minutes, Ryan stood still and moved his eyes just as Mrs. Savant did when trying to find me a seat. Actually, he was making sure that not a soul was in earshot.

"Okay," he whispered, "if we're going to make her a witch, she's going to observe many nights of witchcraft, starting tonight."

"But how's she going to get permission to go out of the house at midnight?" asked Karen.

I wanted to join in the conversation, but thought it would be better to keep quiet.

"We *could* sneak her out of her house at around eleven . . . *hmmm* . . . let's say . . . eleven fifty-five," suggested Ryan.

"No, too risky," Karen disagreed, as she fiddled around with her amethyst, which she had taken from her pocket. "We could just *ask* her parents for permission for her to be out with us till one."

"Oh right, like *that* would work!" Phanny laughed. "What're you gonna say? 'Mr. and Mrs. Romero, could we take Allison to the woods at twelve to watch us do witchcraft?'"

"Oh, and I suppose you can think of something *better,* huh?"

"You bet I can!"

"All right, let's hear it," she said in a challenging voice, still toying with her tiny amethyst.

Phanny stared at Karen, who was crossing her arms, waiting for an answer, then began, "We shouldn't do something that would get her into trouble, or ask her parents for something that would surely be answered with a 'no,' *right?* So we could just make up an alibi for her to be out of the house—without her parents knowing that she'll be in the woods learning witchcraft."

"Such as . . . ?" asked Karen and Ryan together, getting interested.

"Such as a sleep-over. I could pretend that I'm having a sleep-over, which Allison is invited to. You know, as a warm welcome. *Then,* at eleven fifty-five, we'll go to the woods, where she will observe a whole night of potion-making, spells, and old-time witchcraft."

The other two looked at her in total amazement. I was quite pleased with her plan, too.

"Okay!"

"That's great!"

"Yeah!"

We all gushed out a word or two of agreement, still amazed at what Phanny had come up with. She looked at us one-by-one, then smiled, looking pleased with herself as well.

"Okay," whispered Phanny, now facing me, "we'll walk with you all the way home, then we'll wait outside. You go in and ask your parents to come outside and meet us. Then we'll take it from there."

I rubbed my chin, then hesitantly mumbled, "How are you going to convince them to let me go?"

Phanny laid a hand on my shoulder and assured me in her normal voice, "Trust me, we'll convince them."

Suddenly, my stomach growled. They all looked at me. "What? I'm starved! Has the school ever heard of *lunch?*"

We walked and walked, and before we knew it, we were at my door. I twisted the knob to check if it was unlocked. The door opened as I pulled the knob. When I stepped in, I shut the door, and walked to the kitchen, sensing that my parents would be there. Sure enough, when I arrived, into the huge kitchen, my parents were taking a break from unpacking.

"What did you do at school today?" asked my mom.

"Met new friends?" shouted my dad from the far end of the kitchen.

"Yeah, I mean yes. In *fact,* they're outside, waiting to meet you."

"Oh *really?*" they asked together.

"Really."

"Oh, *really?*"

"Really."

"Oh, come now," said my mom. "What kid in his or her right mind would want to meet *us?*"

"Mom, really, they're out there. Go check. Besides, you two are the coolest parents in the world!" (I hit the perfect note there!)

"Well, if you put it *that* way.... Okay then, let's meet them," agreed my mom, finally accepting the fact that I had friends outside, waiting to meet them. We walked to the door and opened it.

"Oh, hello!" cried my mom in feigned delight, "You must be Allison's friends." I walked to where Phanny and Karen stood, which was behind Ryan.

"Yes, we are, Mr. and Mrs. Romero," Ryan talked in an innocent way. "How are you two on this *lovely* afternoon?"

"We're fine, young lady—oh—I meant—I'm so sorry—young *man*."

"It's all right, ma'am, it happens," he said through gritted teeth. He went very pink, and Phanny, Karen, and I chuckled from behind. When we stopped, he introduced himself, and the two other girls. "Yes, well, my name is Ryan, and these two are Karen and Phanny."

"You all have very beautiful *first* names," smiled my mom, "but none of you are Madonna. How about some last names?"

"Oh yes. My name is Ryan *Nakano,* and this is—"

"My name is Karen Tran," she interrupted, putting her amethyst into her pocket. "It's a pleasure to meet you!"

"And my name is Phanny Soi," followed Phanny. "Spelled S-O-I. Pronounced *sigh.*"

The both of them smiled mockingly at Ryan. In a feeble voice, Ryan continued, "There you go. Now we're acquainted with one another." He stepped back a little, as if he were giving room for someone else to talk. Phanny and Karen nudged him hardily in the ribs, then gave false coughs. He gave a sigh and stepped forward again.

"Phanny's having a sleep-over tonight, and your daughter is invited. You know, a welcome to the new neighborhood."

"If Phanny's having the sleep-over, then why are *you* asking us?" asked my dad eyeing him suspiciously.

"She's just a little timid. She doesn't have real good social health. Doesn't get out much, you know." He then whispered, *"Anxiety."* Ryan struggled to keep his lips tight together, on the verge of laughing. *"Ouch!"* Phanny had socked him on the back.

"He's just joking around. Friends. They'd tease you

too." Phanny laughed, then added, "I'll be glad to take her to school in the morning."

"Hmmm," pondered my mom. "What do *you* think, Daddy?" She faced my dad.

Hold on for a minute. Let me explain a little something about Filipino parents. You see, usually, they call each other things like *Daddy, Dad, Papa, Mommy, Mom, Mama, Ma,* you know, the names their children would call them. My mom calls my dad *Daddy,* and my Dad calls my mom *Ma.* Okay, just wanted to let you know.

He nodded. "As long as it's a *girls'* night only." He eyed Ryan. (Man, these Filipino fathers!)

"What, *him?*" asked Phanny, jerking her thumb at Ryan. "Oh, don't worry about him! He's as much of a girl as any of us!" Phanny bit her lip, trying to keep it shut. "Ow!" Ryan crushed her foot.

"Would it be fine then, Mrs. Romero? Sir?" asked Ryan, as Phanny pranced around in the background.

"Okay, I guess she could go," replied my mom when my dad shrugged.

"Thank you, Mrs. Romero, Mr. Romero," said Karen.

"My mom will pick her up around seven-thirty, if that's all right?" added Phanny, secretly (yet not secretly enough for me) plucking out a few hairs off Ryan's head.

"Oh, yeah, that'll be fine!"

"Okay, see you tonight, Allison!"

"Bye!" they all called.

"Bye, guys!" I yelled back.

After shutting the door, I zoomed up to my room. I took out my empty backpack and started packing up. This time, I planned to wear black to school. For school, I packed up a knee-length solid black skirt, a cute black blouse, and casual black dress shoes. I decided to pack some black flare jeans, and a black sweater for this night.

The only colors of pajamas I had were navy blue, true blue, and sky-blue. Of course, I chose to pack the darkest blue ones.

After I had finished packing, I went down to the kitchen for a snack. I walked in, and there, cooling on the table, was a tray of freshly baked cookies. Since I was starving to death for not having lunch, I reached out for one. Smack! A spatula slapped my hand.

"*Ow!*"

"Don't you have some homework to be done, *anak?*" It was my mom.

"Not at this school!"

"Is that so?" she eyed me suspiciously.

"Uh, huh. And they don't have lunch, either."

"Oh, *really?*"

I nodded. She stared into my eyes for a while, then finally said, "All right, take *one.*"

I reached out again and gladly grabbed a warm cookie, then poured myself a glass of cold milk. Ah, it tasted more delectable knowing that the rest of the day was free time for me. My tongue savored each morsel as the chocolate chunks slowly melted away. When I had gulped down the last drop of milk, I decided to walk through the woods and listen to the serene melody of my surroundings in solitude. This truly was my perfect day!

Six
Lazy Day

Once I walked into the woods, I was in a trance. I spun around as the leaves showered on me. With one swift move, I untied my hair and let it sway with the wind. The whole day was mine, and I wanted my day to be lazy! With a free, light heart, I jumped into a large pile of leaves. I was only getting started.

I raced past the trees and breathed in the sweet air. All I could do was laugh as I skipped and danced around like a little child without a single care in the world. For a while, I lay on a long flat stone, gazing out through the treetops. I watched the birds flying, clouds passing, and the sky turning pink and orange. After a while, I began to thirst for more freedom.

In a flash, I was up again, being a carefree spirit. I swung on a branch and landed in another huge pile of leaves. As if it were water, I cupped my hands, scooped up the leaves, and threw them up. They showered back down on me. I laughed and sighed like a child who didn't know the word "worry." I closed my eyes. The wind sighed with me. It sang with me. It was lazy with me. It blew on my face and brushed through my hair. Into my ears, it whispered, "Be free, my beautiful song-bird. Fly!"

With that, I spread out my arms and I let the wind sweep me away! How free I felt! I just stood there, my arms spread out. The wind felt like freedom against my face. Deeply, I inhaled the cool, crisp air. All of Mother Nature's creations swirled around me. I smiled and laughed for no reason at all.

Again, I lay down on the stone, watching the sky deepen. I lay there till I saw the blue crescent moon in the sky.

Seven
The Feigned Sleep-Over

At around six, I headed back for home. "I'm home!" I yelled blissfully after unlocking the door. I felt that all the stress had melted out of me when I was at the woods. There was no reply, so I yelled again, "I'm *ho-ome!*" Still, there was no answer. I suddenly went silent, straining my ears for the slightest sound. . . .

"*Aaahhh!*" I heard a shrill shriek of a woman. I listened again. "*Eeehhh!*" another piercing scream came from a distant room. It sounded exactly like my mom! I ran through the living room, and into the family room. There, standing on the couch, was my frantic mom. She was staring down at a forest-green frog on the floor, clinging onto my dad.

"Ma," he said, "I can't get the frog if you don't let go of me!"

"Take it away, oh, *please* take it away!" screamed my mom.

"Hold on, Mrs. Romero, we've got it," assured Ryan, who was standing next to my parents.

Phanny and Karen were right behind the frog. Karen was holding a clear plastic fishbowl, partially filled with water. She placed the bowl on a table next to her, took out her amethyst, and rubbed it lightly as she stared at the frog, attentively.

"Got it!" they shouted together, flinging themselves to the floor. A loud *thud!* made the frog leap with fright to the other end of the room.

"I was gonna get it!" complained Phanny. "You were supposed to hold the bowl!"

"You took forever! Besides, you wouldn't have caught it anyway!"

"Would so!"

"*Sure, Phanny.*"

"I *really* would have!"

"Um, girls," squeaked my mom, "could you please stop quarreling and capture that frog!"

The frog leapt to a corner of the room. I ran towards it, "I'll get it, Mom, don't worry!" When I got to it, it was cornered. "Gotcha!" I exclaimed, lightly pinning it down. "Karen, get me the bowl!" She rushed it to me, then I dropped in the frog.

I could tell that my mom was relieved, because she jumped to the floor and sighed, "Oh, thank you! Thank you!"

"What did I tell you, Mrs. Romero? I told you we'd get it under control," Ryan said, looking rather proud of himself.

Karen, Phanny, and I looked at him incredulously, "*We?* So what did *you* do?"

The arrogance and boldness of superiority in Ryan's face flushed into a crimson balloon.

I smiled, then talked through the corner of my mouth, "So, Karen . . . what's with the frog?"

"It's for a potion," she mumbled back.

"Potion? What potion?"

"We're going to make a potion, and other things, you know, to demonstrate a bit of our knowledge of witchcraft to you."

"If you're making a potion, then what does the frog have to do with it?"

"I'd rather not tell you. You'll find out later, though."

"Are you ready?" Ryan asked, his face restored to its original state.

"Huh? Oh—yeah, um, I'll get my stuff, but aren't you just a bit—"

"Too early?" he finished. "Oh, we know. Phanny's mom is inviting all of us to dinner. Wanna go?"

"Sounds good, Ally, you should go," recommended my mom, who was sitting smugly on a rocking chair. I could tell she just did not want to cook.

I saw that they were waiting for my reply. "All right," I said slowly, "let me just gather my stuff." I rushed up the stairs, broke into my room, and grabbed my bag. Before I went out, though, something crossed my mind: I hadn't told Ryan and the others about my dream yet.

"Ally." My mom had walked in. "Your friends are waiting for you outside."

"*Hmmm?* Oh, okay, I'll be out."

As she walked out, I mounted the pack onto my back. I looked out the window and saw that they were waiting for me. Since I did not want to be an inconvenience by keeping them waiting, I ran out my door and went down the stairs. When I got outside, I rushed down to the 1987 burgundy Toyota Tercel that Phanny was leaning against.

"Finally!" she shouted, looking annoyed. "My mom kept murmuring things like 'this is taking forever!' or 'why did I agree to this.' It's driving me insane!"

"Well, I'm here! So . . . do we go in, or—"

"My mom will drive us until your house is out of sight, then we'll have to walk the rest of the way."

"What?! Why?"

"Because she said *normal people* annoy her! I'll be honest, *she's* the annoying one! She is-is so-so-so . . . *irritating!*" she exclaimed, trying to find the right word.

"You don't find that offensive, do you?" asked Ryan, looking at me.

"What?"

"Her mom considers you as a *normal* person."

I furrowed my eyebrows in bewilderment. "Why would I be offended? I'm not a witch, so what?"

"So you *don't* find that offensive?"

"Of course not! Is it not okay to be unfamiliar with witchcraft?"

"Of course it's okay."

"Right. But of course, she does not have to *like* me, because I know she doesn't."

"Oh well, you'll be a witch soon," assured Ryan quietly. "She'll get a liking to you then." Ryan held his hand out towards the inside of the car, "Step inside."

"You know, Ryan," I pointed out, "ever since you met my parents, you've been polite. What gives?"

"Good first impressions are what make people fond of you," he replied talking through the corner of his mouth.

"Then why are you doing this for me now?"

"Your parents are at the window."

I looked back. They were. Watching us, their arms around each other's shoulders, as if thinking, *"Yes!* We have the whole night to ourselves!!"

"*Bootlicker!*" I mumbled to Ryan, then I stepped into the car. We drove down a road to the right until the house was out of sight. We suddenly stopped near the woods.

"Don't make any stops on your way home," Mrs. Soi said roughly to her daughter. "Dinner will be on the table."

"Okay!" answered Phanny, very agitated as we

walked out. Once I got out and slammed the car door shut, the car zoomed farther down the road.

"She's not a very hospitable mother, is she, Phanny?" I asked.

"You should see the family," she mumbled.

When we finally arrived at her house, 2091 Tsan Lane, Phanny took out a shiny silver key. She unlocked the door and went inside. "I'm home!" she yelled.

"Who cares?!" I heard a voice reply, probably from the dining room.

"My sister," informed Phanny.

"What did your mom cook this time?" asked Ryan, teasingly. "Not Cream of *Cardboard* again, is it?"

"It was *not* cardboard, it was chicken."

"*Sure it was.*"

"It *really* was!"

"What are you talking about?" I interrupted.

"Well, the last time I came over for dinner, her mom cooked soup that had chunks of cardboard in it."

"*Chicken!*"

"Yeah, yeah, whatever."

"Ooh, yummy!" I joked.

As we ate dinner, I ate in very small portions, because sure enough, it tasted like cardboard. We were eating what seemed to be flaky cardboard pancakes covered in watered down gravy.

The table was noisy. Phanny's sisters were chattering their jaws away, her mom was gossiping over her cell phone, and her dad and what seemed to be a friend, were roaring with laughter. Phanny turned scarlet with embarrassment.

"I'm so sorry it's so loud," she yelled over the head-pounding din, "but it's like this every time I have guests. They always dislike them for some stupid reason, and think making noise annoys them."

"Your family has no hospitality at all!" mumbled Karen, pampering a headache.

"*I know!*" Phanny groaned. We all looked at her, our expressions indicated that we wanted to get away from the noise. "Let's go upstairs." The three of them eagerly stood up, but I stayed put, minding my manners.

"Don't you have to ask to be excused from the table?" I asked.

"Not if you're a Soi. We—well, actually—*they* believe politeness is for *normal* people. It's stupid, but that's the way they take politeness."

For nearly five hours, we played chess and Scrabble. I found that very enjoyable. Karen would always rub the bluish-purple stone in her hand on her moves, and somehow, ended up making good ones, winning every game. I then figured that the stone was for good luck.

"Hey," said Ryan, "what's that on your shoulder?"

"Oh, that? It's just a birthmark."

"Not *just* a birthmark!" exclaimed Phanny. "It looks like a serpent!"

"I know. I've been insisting to my parents that it meant something, but after so many years of convincing, well, I'm convinced."

They kept marveling at it, as if it were a giant diamond, rather than a birthmark.

"Guys," I looked at them, one eyebrow cocked, "It's just a birthmark."

"Uhem, right." said Ryan.

"Now, who want's to challenge me in a game of chess?" I challenged.

A while later, Phanny looked at the clock. "Let's go!"

she called, looking quite awake. It was eleven fifty-five, and I was exhausted! "What's the matter?" she asked me.

"I'm beat! It's way past my sensible bedtime."

"Well, get used to it, you'll be doing this more often."

I rubbed my eyes wearily. "I don't think I can live through this!"

Eight
Witches' Night Out

We walked through the woods until we got to a circular area that was clear from trees. The sound of nearby covens talking and chanting hummed in the air. I saw Ryan pulling something out from a bush. What I saw was so beautiful and attractive, that when I laid eyes upon it, I couldn't take them off. It was a crystal blue cauldron. My eyes sparkled at the sight of its gleaming appearance.

"Like it?" asked Ryan, seeing my pleased eyes.

"Where did you get it?" I asked in awe.

"My sister."

"Wow! Really? That's more than generous of her to give such a cauldron!"

"Give? Who said anything about her giving it to us? We stole it!"

I raised my eyebrows. "*Stole?* You *stole* it?"

"Yeah," he replied plainly.

I was a little shocked. For a while, I said nothing, then I asked, "How did you get away with it?"

"Well, I smuggled it out of her room the night before she moved to college. She and a few friends went out, and she never found out about the loss until the next afternoon."

"How did she find out?"

"She called us when she arrived at the airport. I

asked my mom to let me talk to her. I taunted her quietly over the phone until she hung up. She was really ticked off, but I couldn't see why, knowing she wouldn't be needing the thing anyway."

"Okay," said Phanny, clapping her hands briskly. "Less tales, more spells, people!"

"Right!" remembered Ryan. "Um . . . Allison, please get some firewood so we can get started."

"Okay." I headed into the trees. In about five minutes, I came back with a bundle of wood cradled in my arms. "Would this be all right?"

"That would be fine," panted Ryan, who had been dragging the cauldron to the center. "Just get the stand and put the cauldron over it."

I walked over to the cauldron and set the wood to the side. I saw something that was made of rusty metal rods beside the bush-of-a-hiding place. The top rod was curved into a circle, and three straight rods, about a foot each, were welded to the bottom of it. Though its hideous appearance didn't compare to the gleaming cauldron, I figured it must have been the stand.

Knowing this, I took it over to the cauldron and tried lifting the large pot. It was heavier than I thought. The more I tried lifting, the more it got heavy. After my sixth attempt to lift, I gave up. This cauldron was just too heavy.

Phanny came up to me and gave me a hand, "Need any help?" I just looked at her. She looked determined, so I let her by. Without a hitch, she lifted it as if she was opening the trunk of a car. After that, she mounted it onto the rusty stand. Like Ryan at the car door, she outstretched her arms, presenting the ground. "Go ahead," she said, "place the wood here."

I took the bundle of wood and placed it under the stand. "Okay," I said. "What now?"

"Just sit on that log over there," answered Ryan. He was pointing at a log that was about ten yards from the cauldron. "Observe our every move. Look at the ingredients we use, listen to our chants. Try remembering what we do tonight, and jot down notes if necessary. You *do* have a notepad, right?"

"Well, no. I didn't know I had to—"

"Then take mine," he interrupted. He handed me a suede-bound notepad, a beautiful sky-blue quill, and a tiny bottle of silvery-blue ink. I was surprised that he gave me a fine plumed quill and gorgeous colored ink, because I just expected a simple pencil.

"Wow! Where did you get this? Also from your sister?"

"No." He laughed. "I got it from my dad. It had been passed down from his side of the family since the time of the Salem Witch Trials. The bottle of ink seems to be bottomless, or possibly . . . automatically refillable."

He looked at my expression. Seeing that I looked rather impressed, he smiled slyly. I could tell that he knew that this was a perfect time to make me interested in false stories about himself.

"Well, you *know,*" he started, trying vainly to sound casual, "it's said that every Nakano has some special abilities, and mine happened to be being courageous and defensive against dark magic, and of course, we're always a charmer." He smiled an I'm-so-great smile. Trying to be more impressive, he stretched out his hand and shifted his body to lean against a tree next to him. Before I could tell him that the tree was not accurately beside him, he was on the ground. In other words, he tried leaning on a tree but fell flat on the ground instead.

I rolled my eyes with a smile, on the brim of laughter. When I lowered my eyes to look at him, he lay face down on the mat of dead leaves. Blocking the fact that the situation was amusing to me, I let out a sigh and reached out for him.

"Need any help?"

He slowly craned his neck to face me, and gave me an embarrassed smile. In a feeble voice, he said, "Oh-ha! Um—meant to do that!"

I started to giggle. He was as red as a ripened apple. After slowly getting to his feet, he laughed at himself, trying to feel a little less embarrassed by his fall. "That *was* a bit funny, wasn't it?" he laughed.

"The night doesn't last forever, you two!" nagged Karen. "Let's get to some serious business!"

"Okay," said Ryan soberly.

"Oh, by the way, Ryan," called Phanny.

"Yeah?"

"Could you get some water for the potion?" She was holding out a wooden bucket.

"Sure." He grabbed the bucket and disappeared into the curtain of trees. In a few minutes, he returned. "Here you go."

"Oh . . . thank you," Phanny sounded disappointed. As Ryan turned to walk away, she asked, "Ryan, could you get two more buckets of water, please?"

"Oh, okay." He didn't sound as willing as the last time. After dumping the first bucket of water into the cauldron, Phanny gave him back the bucket. When he returned, he poured the water into the cauldron, and went off once more. Before he could tip the bucket over the cauldron the third time, he looked at Phanny with a face I guessed meant that he was expecting another task.

"Oh, Ryan," Phanny started. Ryan hunched his back, angrily dropping the whole bucket into the cauldron. "Could you hand me the spell book?"

"*Sure,*" answered Ryan through gritted teeth. He picked

up an old worn out book with a dusty leather binding. It looked just like the one from the dream! "Here you go."

Come to think of it, I thought, *I haven't told them about the dream yet.* This suddenly came in my mind when Phanny asked Ryan to do something again. It was humorous and amusing to watch them, so I continued to keep silent and watch them, which I truly regret nowadays. I always think of all those times I had to tell them about the dream. I could have saved Ryan, Howie—he, most especially—and myself, from our horrid fate. . . .

"Ryan, could you hand me the ingredients?"
"*Yeah.*"
"Also, Ryan, could you help me read this spell?"
"*Okay.*"
"Oh, and Ryan—"
"**WHAT!!!**" he barked.
"Um, you—have some—some leaves—from—from when you fell."
"Oh, he—he, right." He turned pink, and started brushing the front of his coat.

Soon, I was sitting on the log, observing them while taking notes. As I watched them do a healing potion, I thought I heard something rustling in the bushes behind me. *It's probably the wind,* I thought to myself, without turning.

They were going to do their fourth spell, which was for good luck, when I decided to reread my notes.

Notes

I. Keep quiet during spells or potion-making unless necessary.
II. Love spell

    A. Wine glass
    B. Small amount of red wine
    C. Crushed cinnamon
    D. Red rose petals (fresh or dry)
        1. Pour wine in glass; say, "With this may my lover come."
        2. Add petals; say, "I charge this spell with the rose of love and passion to awaken my soul mate."
        3. Add cinnamon; "With this may the aroma awake him (or her)."
        4. Hold up the glass; say, "Awake!"
        5. Drink a sip and save the rest in another bottle.
III. A frog is a common ingredient for magic potions.

I stopped to think of that. The moment I saw Phanny drop that frog into the simmering pot, I paled, sickened. No wonder Karen didn't want to tell me about it. I continued, not wanting to waste time.

IV. Dried herbs and spices are very essential for potions.
    A. Cinnamon
    B. Bay Leaves
    C. Ground Ginger
    D. Marjoram
    E. Ground Cloves
    F. Basil
    G. Rosemary
    H. Sage
V. Say your incantations clearly.

After skimming through the notes, I looked back at the three. Ryan walked in between the other two, holding the tattered spell book. He opened it and held it with his right hand, turning the pages with his left. I saw him stop on a page. Wanting to copy down the page number and title into my notes, I jumped to my feet and tip-toed, hoping to get a glimpse of the page.

Ryan looked at Karen, then at Phanny. They nodded to each other. *Was this a part of the spell?* I thought to myself. The three of them faced me, and Ryan glided smoothly towards me. Without a sound, he showed me the page and allowed me to copy it down.

After I finished, I tried to thank him, but before my mouth could move, he pressed his finger against his lips; a silent gesture for silence. After that, they all repositioned and continued with the spell.

Oh, so he just wanted to show me the page, it wasn't a part of the spell. Although, I could have sworn that he didn't see me tip-toeing from his position, and my lips didn't do as much as to quiver when he warned me not to talk. On the other hand, I probably *did* move my mouth a bit, and Ryan *could* have seen me through the corner of his eye as I struggled to see that page. Those *were* logical possibilities for his pre-knowledge of my actions, but he looked so focused with what they were doing . . .

I saw that Ryan was once again, holding the book with his right hand. They were going to start the spell. Quickly, I picked up the notepad and quill, ready to write, like a reporter, interviewing someone. The three of them started reading the spell. Ryan was motioning his arms like a madman as they did.

[*]"By Horned God, Crescent Lady, Stable Earth, Moving Air, Energetic Flames, Serene Waters, Mysteri-

---

[*]*Good Luck Spell,* by Ryan Trinh

ous Akasha. By North, South, East, West, and Center. By Salamanders, Sylphs, Gnomes, and Undines. By Djinn, Paralda, Nichsa, and Ghob. Raphael, Gabriel, Michael, and Auriel. I call upon the four watchtowers, the four watchers, and the quartet of elements. Come to bring me good luck. Blessed be."

They had already finished, but I was still writing down the words in the notepad. When I finally finished, Phanny approached me with a little bit of weariness in her eyes.

"We should go now." She yawned. "It's two-thirty in the morning."

"I think so too," I agreed in a larger yawn.

After Ryan had stored the cauldron back into the bushes, he and Karen went to their own homes. Phanny and I went to her house. I still had to pretend to be at a sleepover. That was all for the night, yet it wasn't all for the rest of my life, for the rest of the other nights to come would be more than jotting down a few notes.

Nine
Allison Romero: Witch's Apprentice

Have you ever wondered what it was like to be a witch's apprentice? Well, it's sort of great, but it sure is a sore job! Here are a few examples of a few of my training nights:

Saturday, May 19, 2001

"Okay Allison," said Karen, "you're sure you fully know the shielding spell?"

"Yeah, I'm sure."

Ryan stood a few yards ahead of me. He extended his arms to the sky and bellowed, "Patior furor d'Zeus!"

"Defendo!" I bellowed, pointing a finger at Ryan.

All of a sudden, I was struck by lightning, and I mean *lightning,* because of course, "Patior furor d'Zeus," means, "Suffer the wrath of Zeus"—which of course is to get struck by lightning.

I just stood there, eyes shocked, finger still pointing, and my whole body charred and smoking.

"You got the word correct," said Karen. "But first of all, because you are protecting yourself from something, you're supposed to use your hands. Second of all, you're supposed to hold up your hands in the air. You're blocking yourself from lightning, not Ryan." She looked at me as if I were a pathetic, lost puppy, shaking her head.

Phanny came up to my face. "Uh, Allison?"

"*Oh, okay,*" I managed to puff out.

Friday, May 25, 2001

I stopped stirring the contents of the cauldron to take off my wig, revealing what the lightning incident had left me: a bald head. "So, Ryan," I asked, "grounded peach stones, vinegar, maiden hair, white wine, and Aconite would grow my hair back, right?"

Ryan replied, "Mhmm . . . wait! What was that last one?!"

"A–a–aconite," I repeated worriedly.

"*Aconite?* As in *wolf's bane? Oh, no!*" asked Phanny fearfully.

"What?" I asked nervously.

The liquid bubbled furiously in the cauldron, then suddenly burst out. I fell back. The eruption continued for a few seconds, then stopped in an instant.

I looked up and saw the three, smiling—almost laughing—at me.

"What?" I demanded.

Phanny tried not to laugh, "Heh, well, at least we know it works!"

"It worked?!" I exclaimed, touching my head, becoming disappointed again. "I'm still bald!"

"I—I don't think that's what Phanny—ha, ha—m—meant," Karen said, also trying not to laugh.

I looked at them puzzled.

"Allison," said Ryan. He was scratching his chin.

"Huh?" I touched my own chin. My eyes widened.

"AAAAAAAAAAAAAAAAAAAAAAAAAAAAAAAA AAH!!!"

On my chin, was a yard-long beard!

Sunday, May 27, 2001

"Now," said Ryan, "I'm going to test you on potions and enchanted ointments. You will either have to tell me the name of the potion or ointment, where its recipe is, or a brief description of it. Ready?"

I deeply inhaled and said, "Yes."

"Okay. What potion makes hollow butterfly vapor formations when opened?"

I thought for a moment, then answered, "A reverie potion!"

Ryan smiled and gladly said, "Correct. Where would you find the recipe of *Sorcerer's Choice* healing potion?"

After some thought, I answered, *"Marvin Marsh's Marvelous Book of Healing for Young Witches and Warlocks,* chapter three, page three fifty-four!"

"That's right! Okay, Give me a brief description of the reverie potion."

"It forms butterfly vapor formations, it's a translucent baby-blue, and would make whoever drinks it have a sort of dreamy slumber—like sleeping gas."

He shook his head smiling. "You just keep on surprising me!"

Phanny and Karen stood quietly, fairly apart from us. Phanny was smiling broadly, but Karen was crossing her arms, frowning at me. Why didn't she like it when I was correct? She didn't even like it when I wasn't correct!

Ryan then asked, "What potion makes you fly? The

levitating potion does not count, and it's not called a flying potion."

I was stuck there. I knew they could tell I was. Ryan stared at me intently, Phanny was biting her lip, and Karen rolled her eyes. "Um . . ."

"Well?"

"Oh . . ."

"Time counts as well," added Ryan.

I started to perspire. "I . . ."

"Ten . . . nine . . . eight . . ."

"Ah . . ."

"Five . . . four . . . three . . ."

"**RED BULL!**"

Ryan looked down and shook his head, disappointedly. Phanny slapped her forehead. Karen smirked.

"Sorry," said Ryan. "*Potio d'Avis,* or *Potion of the Bird,* is the correct answer. Energy drinks don't count, Allison."

"*It gives you wings,*" I timidly said.

He shook his head.

Wednesday, May 30, 2001

"Now," said Ryan, "let's see how much power you can summon to your own body and how you use it."

"Oh, whoa . . . okay." I was nearly going to faint.

"Okay, Allison, deep breath, deep breath. . . ."

As I inhaled the crisp night air, I looked at each of them. Phanny looked encouraging, Ryan hopeful . . . but there was Karen. Karen was crossing her arms, a this-is-pointless-she's-hopeless-anyway look on her face.

Trying to erase that face, I concentrated with all my might. I closed my eyes, raised up my hands, and concentrated. Power like nothing I'd ever experienced before began to buzz into me. It was an odd sensation.

Just as I was beginning to believe that it was going to turn out great, a powerful jolt shot me into the trees.

Karen sneered, her expression saying, "I told you so!"

Phanny and Ryan ran towards me, looking feverishly worried. "Are you okay?!" they asked.

Their voices came from farther and further away. Just as I was about to black out, I heard Karen say, "Why are we wasting our time for such a stupid, *hopeless* girl?! We might as well be teaching a dog . . ."

So you see, the next time someone asks *you* to become a witch's apprentice, just say, "No thanks, stay away from me!" Then run, run, **RUN!!!**

Ten
Our Gigantic Problem

Like the first night of observing, the following observing nights meant staying up until two-thirty in the morning. I always tried my best to make my observing/training nights weekends. If not, I came home from school, not knowing what to say when my parents asked, "What did you learn at school today?" That's because I went to school ready to sleep, thanks to the long night before, which was when I'd do simple spells, counter-curses, and potions, as well as jotting down notes.

It was Thursday, June the seventh, which meant I'd been training for over a month now. I had been going to the woods once a week, striving to make up better alibis each time to do so. On this day, all I had to do was to study my notes and the witchcraft books I had hidden under my bed. On the next night, I would be taking a witchcraft test. If I passed, I would be proven witch-worthy and be part of Ryan's coven.

The time was three o' clock, after school. Karen, Phanny, and I were waiting for Ryan at the front of the school building. I was distressed. Something seriously horrible was bothering me. I didn't want to tell Ryan about it. The matter of it would have probably alarmed him.

I overheard Jenny and her group talking about Ryan.

Earlier, I had been walking out of math class, when I heard their voices coming from a corner near the restrooms. Let me flash back and give you a glimpse of what happened.

The racket of the school bell rang around nine o' clock, and the classes poured into the halls. Just as I walked out, I heard Jenny's voice say something about Ryan. I followed her voice, and saw her and her lot. They were standing in front of the girls' restroom, next to a row of lockers. I hid behind the door of an opened locker.

". . . Ryan and his coven are trying to get that Allison girl into their coven," said Jenny in a slightly quiet voice.

"That stupid oaf's trying to get her into his coven?" exclaimed Tay. "But she's not even a witch!"

"They've been training her to be a witch since she came. I found out on the first night Allison's spent observing witchcraft. While I was waiting for you three, I decided to spy on Ryanna, Amethyst Girl, and Fony. I saw that wanna-be witch sitting on a log. I was going to put a amnesiac spell on her so she couldn't remember who she was or what she was doing, when you tapped me. I accidentally made the bush I was hiding behind rustle. So that explains why I rushed you three away. Lucky for you, the pip-squeak didn't turn around."

"Is she going to be taking the witchcraft test any time soon?" asked Tay.

"She's scheduled to take the test tomorrow!"

"So Ryan and his coven are trying to outdo us or something?" asked a light-complexioned Mexican girl with glasses and thick brown hair.

"Yeah," said Jenny in a confident voice, "but I doubt she'll pass. Am I right, Kris?" She faced the girl. She must have been Krystine Mendoza.

"And if she *does?*" said another girl, who was tan and

had smooth dark hair, which was shoulder length. I figured that she must be Katrina Santiago. She was, like me, Filipina.

"She won't, I tell you!"

"But—" Tay began.

"*Look,* I have a plan. You know that only the leader could give you the test. You know, you have to stop the leader from cursing you, and you have to do a counter-curse, blah, blah, blah?" The three nodded. "Well, since that's the case, all we have to do is *kill* Ryanna!"

"*Kill?!* But that's a felony!" cried Tay. The other two looked alarmed.

Jenny replied casually, "So it is, isn't it? Oh well, it's nothing we can't get away with. Besides, we're evil geniuses, right?"

"I guess you're right," replied Tay. "But how?"

"When he—maybe at—oh, I'll think of something."

My jaws dropped. They're planing to *kill* Ryan! *This couldn't be good,* I thought. Suddenly, a large kid came along and bumped into the locker door, slamming me inside.

"Help! Can someone help—"

Oh, he-he. How much of that did you read? Well, never mind that part. Throughout the day, I perspired in class, thinking of the worst.

As Mister Boris talked about death and bloodshed in his war stories, the words "Ryan's dead!" flashed into my mind. The same thing happened when Miss Nightingale read about the time Odysseus impaled Polyphemos's eye with a white-hot sword from Homer's *The Odyssey.*

I kept a close watch on the time, wishing that the day would be over. *Bong! Bong! Bong! Bong!* To my relief, the inferno din of the school bell ended after sixth period. I was never so grateful to hear its annoying ring. In a flash,

I was out the gym door, still in my gym clothes. As the flood of students covered me, I jumped up to the surface of the sea, wanting to find Phanny and Karen so that I could pour out all the information. When I saw them walking down the stairs, I dashed towards them.

"What's the matter?" they both asked when I clung onto the scruff of Phanny's black turtleneck at the bottom of the stairs, catching my breath.

"Tell you . . . out . . . side" I panted, shoving them out the front door. In a rush, I told them everything I heard, expecting that they would be worried. Actually, they looked as calm as ever when I had finished.

"Who cares about that girlish idiot?" shouted Phanny.

"Hey, he's the leader of this coven!" I stated defensively.

"So?"

"Well, don't you have any concerns about a fellow witch, well, warlock? I mean, you *are* friends, aren't you? We should spy on Jenny in the woods tonight. She might mention her plan there." I paused, then added, "We've got to keep Ryan from being out in the woods."

Before Phanny could reply, Karen said, "Maybe she's got a point there, Phanny," I saw her wink. I guess she also didn't agree, but just wanted me to stop talking. Pretending I didn't see her, I looked at Phanny as I listened to Karen. "I say we spy on Jenny tonight and tomorrow night until we get an answer. We might have to postpone the test tomorrow, though. Ryan will have to keep out of the woods at night until then, you know. Oh, well, a late test is better than no test, right?"

I played along with the two, although I knew that the joke was on me. Well, that's what happened, at least, it's all you need to know. Now there we were, me, anxiously waiting for Ryan, and Phanny and Karen, watching me from behind. I knew that they were mocking me.

Minutes passed, and eventually, the double-doors swung open. Ryan appeared though the doors, a look of worry sat on his face. *Maybe he found out already.* He walked farther away from the building, not spotting us. It looked as if he were gliding in the air as he strode towards the woods, his eyes wide with fear. He brushed past us.

"*Ryan?*" I asked cautiously.

"Oh, hey!" he said in a surprised voice; he looked shocked. "Look, I think we should postpone the test. I'm guessing you know why." He gave me a suspicious sideways glance.

My stomach made a horrible jolt. *Does he know?* I thought. *If he did, how did he find out? Jenny wouldn't just come up and say that she was going to kill him. No. How did he know that I knew? Maybe he had a crystal ball and . . . I'm crazy! My life has been so awkward since that dream.*

"I'm going home. I'll tell you when we'll test you. Go home and stay there. I don't have time now for socializing."

"Well, okay. I'll—I'll go home then," I lied.

He looked at me and gave something that looked somewhat like a frown and a grin. "Liar!" retorted Ryan. "You are going to spy on Jenny, with or without Phanny and Karen. Whatever it takes to prevent her from killing me, *right?*" I just looked at him in shock. *Liar?*

"I know what you're thinking," he hissed, "but you know it's true. You *are* a liar. You said you were going home, but your real thoughts are to do the opposite. You really want to help me. Even though it affects yourself, am I correct?"

"Well, yes," I admitted.

"Great! Then I could stop pretending to be mean. Sorry for calling you a liar, and all that." He started to chuckle, "It just makes it easier."

"It makes *what* easier?" I asked. Now *I* was getting suspicious.

"To see if you know about my special ability, which you obviously don't."

"What do you mean?"

"Oh, come on! Remember that time in the woods? When you needed to see that page? And all those times I finished your sentences before you? How did I know your actions before you even attempted to try? How did I know that you were lying when I told you to go home and stay there. Wouldn't you suggest any reasons?"

"Well, I'm not sure. I thought you saw me through the corner of your eye or something, but—"

"But you did not see my eyes turn. Of course not! I read what was in your mind. I'm telepathic!"

"And so are we," added the other two.

"What! You—you can't be! That's—that's absurd. It's impossible!" I couldn't swallow one bit of this information.

"Oh is it?" He stared into my eyes, his eyes were not those of a prankster. I just stood there in silence, finding this difficult to believe. "Say a short statement in your mind. I'd bet that I would be able to reveal it out loud."

I looked at him, whispered, "You're all mental," then made a statement in my head, positive that he wouldn't know a word of it. "Okay, hotshot, what did I say?"

"Are you sure you want me to say that?"

"What? Are you *afraid* to admit that you are not being truthful yourself? Say it!"

"*Okay,* but I warned you." I was looking at him with my arms crossed. He shrugged.

"You think Jake Stone is the cutest guy in the world!" he laughed.

I blushed. "*Shoo SHUSH!* Okay, okay! I believe you! I *believe* you!" Jake was this boy from math class. You'll meet him later.

"HA! HA! HA! Hey, I should read your mind more often. You have loads of interesting info in this head of yours." He stopped laughing. "*Hmmm . . . you think Harry Potter's real, eh?*"

"Stop that!" I snapped.

"Okay, okay!"

The three started to laugh. To stop the humiliation, I laughed along with them. After a few minutes, we settled down. Something quite confusing to me came into mind.

"Hey, Ryan," I spoke up.

"Yeah?"

"How did you know about me knowing about Jenny's plan, anyway?"

"Well, every time I see anyone with a worried expression, I usually read what's in his or her mind. When I saw you at the gym, you seemed pretty tense, so I ended up finding out about it. I was a little dazed but very concerned about that information, so I made a close watch on Jenny after she came out of the locker room. That's why I came out late. It was a waste though, since I figured out nothing whatsoever about her little plan."

"I *see*," I replied, as something else drifted through my mind. "So tell me, how did you get your telepathic powers?"

He smiled, and started, "Well, it all started when I—"

Oh, wait, wait! Freeze it all! Cut that out of the story! I don't think anyone wants to hear his story. First of all, it took *ages* to conclude, and I don't think anyone wants to hear a story that had nothing to do with how he got telepathic powers. *Unless,* you want to know all about his *Barbie dolls.*

"Allison!"

"Ryan? How did you get here?"

"I do not have dolls!"

Okay, I was just joking around right there. Still, I really don't think you want to hear about things like generic expenses, and psychopathic developments, especially since it wasn't exactly what happened, so he retold the story a million times!

"I only retold it *forty-four* times, and it's *genetic experiments* and *psychological* developments!"

"Whatever, Ryan! Now go back to where you were and freeze!"

All right, just cut out his *long-winded* story. Okay, roll film, oh, right. This is a book. Back to the story!

After Ryan's story, I was only half awake. I half-heartedly (more like half of half) said that his story was interesting, forgetting that he could read my mind. We went back to our original topic.

"I appreciate your awareness." Ryan smiled warmly. "But I don't need your assistance, at least, not yet." I nodded, then I headed for home.

That evening at dinner, I ate in silence, thinking of a possible way in which I could prevent Jenny from harming Ryan. Most of the time, the fork missed my mouth while I stared forward, not blinking at all. It looked as if I had become brainwashed and completely forgotten where my mouth was—and even how to eat.

My parents looked at me as if I were eating like an amphibious creature, and talking in an obscure and indecipherable language. Although I wasn't exactly looking at them, I knew that that was what they thought about as they cautiously watched me.

My mom spoke up, "*Anak,* is something bothering you?"

"Huh? Oh, no. Just thinking of a . . . a story, that . . . that I want to . . . to uh . . . to turn into a book. Um, I got the idea from the woods." This was a lie, but what was I supposed to tell her? Evil witches are out to kill Ryan? No, I couldn't tell them that.

"*Aba!* (An exclamation of awe) That's my girl!" exclaimed my dad, supportively.

"What a bright idea!" followed my mom.

"So . . . when are you planning to start on it?" asked my dad.

"Um, start it? Well . . ." This lie wasn't easy to keep alive, "I guess, next year."

"*Ano?* (What?) Next year?" they both exclaimed, dropping their forks.

"*Bakit* (Why) *next* year?" asked my mom.

"Because, er—because I have to collect more ideas, to uh—make an excellent story line."

"Oh, I *see*," said my mom, picking up her fork. "That's a very *organized* thing to do."

Eleven
The Risk

That night, I tossed and turned through an uneasy slumber. Something woke me up at around eleven o' clock. It might have been my female intuition, or the rustling of the trees outside, but whatever it was said that something was not right. Thinking hard, I thought of a reason of why something should be wrong.

"*Jenny!*" I exclaimed in a whisper, now frantic. *She's going to the woods at midnight, to initiate her plan for Ryan's tragic fate, I just know it!* I suddenly thought. I popped up and headed to my dresser. Changing at such a miraculous speed, I was already dressed before coming to my senses. This time, I didn't have an alibi to be out. *Should I sneak out?* No, what if I got caught? That was a chance I had to take.

With only an hour left before midnight, I decided to make up a few "spy gadgets." I sneaked into the kitchen, and cleverly gathered the essentials: a sports cap, a flash light, a pair of sharp scissors, some string, a thick, strong rubber band, two tough silver forks, scotch tape, plastic sandwich bags, three cans of soda, three packages of Pop Rocks (which is a crackling candy), a mini-pack, and a wrist watch. These and my clever brain were all I needed to make quality gadgets.

With the scissors, I cut a hole through the visor of the

cap. After that, I attached the flashlight by sticking it through the hole in the upturned visor, tying it with the string. I called this gadget, the "nightcap." Lame name, I know, but the use of it is better than its name.

Next, was the "bomb-a-nator." I made three of them. First, I got three cans of soda, three packets of pop rocks, and three sandwich bags. I poured a packet of Pop Rocks into each bag, and taped the mouth of each bag firmly to the top of a can. An interesting piece, I must say. How it worked I won't tell.

I finally got to the third gadget. Using the forks, I made the best weapon a kid could own. Along with the finest rubber band, it was invincible. With a small rubber band, I tied the forks together, forming a "V" shape. After that, I secured the rubber band between each fork, making the finest weapon. (Drum roll) Ladies, gentlemen, and kids, I present to you . . . a slingshot (*Boing! Wock, wock!*).

What? The old *Dennis the Menace* method isn't good enough for you? A slingshot is the best weapon a kid could own! It's portable, easy to hide, and it's simple. You don't think it would work, do you? Well, you'll see! It could save your life one day!

I put the "bomb-a-nators" in the pack, and the slingshot in the back pocket of my jeans.

The only object I haven't explained its purpose for, was the wrist watch. You should know what it's for, do you not? Come on, that's easy to figure out? Do you give up? It's to tell time, of course! People these days!

I wore the watch and checked the time. It was already five to twelve. Trying my best to keep quiet, I crept past the family room and living room. As soon as I reached the door, I slowly twisted the knob. Holding my breath, I walked out the door. When I was out, I carelessly let go of the knob to relieve an itch on my nose. Suddenly, a breeze floated by, and before I could get a grip on the knob, the door slammed shut. I became all the more frantic, but remembering I was doing this for a friend, I put on the "nightcap," switched it on, ran down the driveway, up the rugged dirt path, and into the trees.

I sped deeper into the woods, straining my ears for any sound of conversation. Finally, I heard voices coming towards my direction. Thinking quickly, I hid behind a tree. Being practical, I turned off the flashlight on the cap, as to not blow my cover by shining a bright light at a group of evil witches.

". . . Krystine, keep the potion in your backpack, during gym tomorrow." Jenny was talking to Krystine Mendoza. She wore a black, collared sweater, and a black cotton skirt that hung above her knees.

"All right," she answered.

"Katrina, Tay," she faced Tay, and Katrina Santiago, who wore a gray cashmere turtleneck, and gray and black pants that had a snakeskin pattern.

"We know what to do," they both answered.

"Great!" said Jenny as she clapped her hands once. "It's so simple! Okay, Tay and I will gather the ingredients for the potion. Once he takes the first gulp tomorrow after gym, it's *bye-bye, Ryanna!*"

Sinister laughter rang through the woods. I gasped, then quickly clasped my hand on my mouth (like that would work). Sweat of terror ran down my face, frantic over the fact that they might have heard me.

"Did you hear that?" Katrina heard my gasp.

"Hear what?" asked Krystine.

"I heard some sort of *gasp*. It came from over there," she pointed at the tree where I had been hiding behind.

I shrieked, and without any common sense whatsoever, ran, so as to make the slingshot fling out of my pocket to Jenny and her lot.

"What's this?" Jenny picked up the slingshot. She studied it. "*A homemade slingshot?*" She spun around, searching the trees with her eyes. She called out threateningly, "Whoever you are, I'm going to find you, and when I *do,* you'll be in for the ultimate price!"

I knew very well that she meant death. *It will save your life one day,* mocked a voice in my head. I felt foolish.

Jenny heard the leaves crunching beneath my feet as I ran for dearest life. "There goes the snitch! Don't just stand there, pursue! **PURSUE!**" I was bursting with fear. Suddenly, I got an idea. I took a "bomb-a-nator" out of my pack, shook it vigorously, and tossed it to a boulder with sharp sides, which pierced the can. The soda, along with the pop rocks, fizzed and crackled in a sticky explosion, making a glutinous substance fly at the four girls. It landed on their faces and clung to their hair.

"*Ehhh!*" a shrill shriek came from Katrina, whose face was covered with the gooey "bomb-a-nator" slime.

"Yuck!" yelled Jenny. She took some of the goo with her finger and studied it with disgust. "What the—" she started to say, but stopped, realizing that I was gone. "She, or he—the kid—oh damn!" She was so loud that I could hear her swearing from the middle of the woods. That's where I had run off to. I caught my breath, and continued to run.

It was one o' clock, and I finally reached our driveway. Never was I so glad to see the rocky, sloping asphalt. Like a cat creeping up to pounce on its prey, I peeked through a gap between the curtains. No lights, no parents, the coast was clear.

I cautiously opened the door—which I had carelessly left unlocked when I had left—slid in, and quietly shut the door. Quickly, I moved my eyes around, made sure that no one saw me, and headed towards my room. Through the living room, family room, hallway, and dining room I went, finally reaching the arched entryway leading up the stairs. I trembled and perspired as I tiptoed up the steps, praying I wouldn't meet a soul. *One more step to go . . .*

Creak!

That step made a fortunately faint sound. Relieved, I continued on towards my room. As I laid my hands on the knob, a part of me sensed that something was wrong.

Don't open it, it said.

The other part hissed, *relax, nothing's wrong here. Go on. Besides, you made it here without a hitch, right?*

For a moment, I stood there, debating with my thoughts. Suddenly, I tightened my grip on the door knob, and hastily turned it. *That's it, open the door.*

"*Ahhh!*" I screamed, as the door opened on its own.

"**Allison Juliet Romero, where have you been?**" scolded my mother. He-he, did I tell you I had a *middle* name? "Once we heard that door slam shut, we knew that *something* was wrong!"

"Your mother and I came up here to look for you," yawned my dad. He laid a hand on my shoulder, "Are you all right?" Mom shoved him on the back of his head, making him land face first onto a pillow on my bed.

"Don't ask her questions like that, Daddy!" nagged my mom. "She broke out of the house without our permission!"

"But you don't understand!" I cried abruptly.

"Oh, I understand plenty!"

At these words I became irritated. I lost my cool, and absentmindedly retorted, "You understand nothing, Mother!"

Her face turned purple, and she gave me a nasty look. I tried my best to hide my fears, but they acted like bulls that were peeved and beaten before a bullfight, impatiently banging on the wooden gates. When seeing the look of terror on my face, she loosened up her angry facial expression, drew out some breath, and looked at me square in the eye.

"They're trying to kill Ryan!" I blurted in a shout. "That evil coven and their acrobat friend are going to poison him!"

By now my dad was siting upright, he and my mom were looking at me, their eyebrows reaching for the sky. I just stood there panting. All of a sudden, my mom placed the back of her hand on my forehead frantically.

"Oh, no!" cried my mom. "I told Daddy to search for you. Being outside has gotten you ill! *Oh,* you feel normal. Dad, the thermometer, get the thermometer!"

Dad shot up, and ran out the door. I could hear his footsteps thumping down into the downstairs bathroom, where the medical/first-aid cabinet was.

"Mom, I'm not sick," I said, trying to keep her back. "What I said was true! An evil coven from school is trying to kill Ryan with a magic potion! Oh, Mom, you've got to *believe* me!"

"No! No! No! You have to get some rest. You're making up words—*coven*—what's that? And and—and, a *magic* potion? There was never such a thing!"

"*Mom,* relax. A coven is a group of witches, and—"

"*Witches!*" she shrieked. She then started to sob. "Daddy, call the doctor! It's worse than I thought!"

"In a second, Ma!"

At that point, I felt like exploding. I halfheartedly wanted to tell them the truth about my learning to become a witch, but that would interfere with my chances to even become one. Because of this, I decided to use reverse psychology.

I smiled slyly. "Gee, you're right, Mother, I *am* sick, and I *shouldn't* sneak out like that, especially at night. I should atone for my disobedience. Whatever the punishment is, I deserve it."

"*Deserve it?*" my mom nearly wailed, soaking the thick carpeting with tears. "*Oh, ho, ho, ho!* She *wants* her punishment! Daddy, forget the call, drive her to the emergency room!"

"But, Ma, I just called the—"

"Cancel it! We've got to get her to the hospital now!"

"Dad, don't! Just cancel the call. I'm fine!" I called after him.

"N-n-n-n-n-n-n-No!" she disagreed. "Daddy, get the keys!"

"But—what about—Ally—Ma—I—*ano*?" (what) He became so confused, that he didn't know what to do or say.

This is going to be a long night, I thought to myself. How in the world was I going to end this—this madness?

Twelve
A More Than Queer Morning

The next morning, dawn arose and gave me a warm greeting (and wake-up call), by peeking through my curtains and shining through my eyelids. I woke up with a few blinks and hastily got out of bed, still weary from the previous night.

Settling down this morning's misunderstanding was what I would call a miracle! Around one-thirty, as Mom was dragging me out of my room, I suddenly came up with an idea. Spreading a sly smile on my face, I tugged my wrist from her grasp.

"Mom, Dad," I called their attention, trying to be as casual as possible, "Thanks!"

Mom stopped being worried for a second, and with a puzzled stare, faced me.

"Thanks?" she asked, as if she thought she was hearing things. "Ano'ng (What) *thanks?!*"

"I'm thanking you."

"Oh, *bakit*?" (why) asked Dad.

"You've just gave me a some ideas for my story!"

They looked at each other.

"This," started Mom, "this was all for your story?"

"Of course."

"Then why did you run away?" asked my dad.

"Run away?" I pretended to be confused. "Who said I

ran away?" They looked at each other again. "I let the door slam so you could hear it. After that, I hung around outside. I wanted to see your reactions towards an emergency such as a missing child." I paused, thinking of something to add, just in case if Dad had searched the front for me. "I hid behind a bush with some food."

"But you worried us, *anak*," said Dad, gingerly.

"I'm sorry. I didn't mean to stay out for so long. You see, I fell asleep outside and I just woke up."

They both looked at me, and sighed. "If that's so," said Dad, "then we don't blame you for all this confusion. Just don't do it again, promise?"

I looked at them with a warm smile, and replied, "Promise." They smiled warmly in return, and left me to rest.

Smooth move, huh?

Okay, back to our main topic. After pushing myself out of bed—that's only an expression, because really, I got out of my sleeping bag—I staggered off to the towel closet. I then did my usual morning routine, which meant I brushed my teeth, took a shower, dressed, and ate some breakfast. When I had completed my breakfast of tocino (sweetened pork meat) and rice—a Filipino-styled breakfast—I grabbed my bag and walked out of the door.

It was earlier than usual, but I had the strangest feeling that something was going to slow me down on the way. That was an odd feeling to have, for the morning once again greeted me with its light cool breeze and the wonderful colors that blocked all the dark feelings and thoughts from existing in my mind swirled everywhere. Again, I walked to school in total ecstasy. I felt as if I were in a trance, in which I could feel nothing but joy . . .

"Oof!" I felt myself fall on my back as something collided into me, or maybe I collided with it, I was not sure. I shook myself a bit, and looked up, finding myself staring at Howie Blanks.

"Oops!" he exclaimed, looking as if someone had let a few Rottweilers loose on him. "Err, I'm sorry. I didn't see you, *oh,* I—I wasn't mocking you about your shortness, *eeh—I meant—err, I'm very sorry!*" He looked at my face, and finally realized who I was. Shakily, he said, "Oh, y—you're w—one of R—*Ryan's f—friends,* huh?" He suddenly clasped his hands on my cheeks, "*Don't tell them,* **please** *don't tell them!*"

"I' wasn' yo fot, 'Owie," I said through puckered lips. "Could oo 'elp meh?"

"Oh, right." He took me by the hand and pulled me up. "No, no, you're dusty all over." He started to brush my back with his hands very rapidly.

When he started to comb my hair with his fingers, I felt something cold touch the back of my neck. *Soon after he had finished and retied my hair, I took a glimpse of his hand before he started to search his backpack. I saw on his finger, a ring.* That must have been the cold object that gently stroked my neck.

It was a peculiar looking thing. The band was jet-black and was spiral. On the front, was a silver image of an eye. Wanting to see if there was something else on the eye, I took another look. There, I saw the part of the ring that made it all the more peculiar. In the center of the eye, was a tiny glass sphere representing the pupil of the eye, surrounded by a ruby-red iris. Inside, was gray mist, swirling in the glass. Suddenly, the mist vanished, and the sphere was clear.

I looked at Howie to see if he noticed that I was looking at his ring. When I saw that he was busy uncorking a glass bottle of blood-red liquid with a long neck and a round bottom—which he carefully held with a thickly quilted piece of cloth—I focused my attention on the ring again.

Now, the pupil was blackish-blue. As I continued staring into the tiny glass, an almighty beam shot out of it, stinging my eyes. Quickly, I turned away, simultaneously bending down for my backpack.

"Thanks a lot, Howie," I thanked him as I mounted my bag onto my back. "Don't blame yourself for this. Anyway, it was an accident. Everything's fine."

"Really?" he asked weakly.

I looked at him reassuringly and replied with a smile. "Really."

He gave me a feeble smile, then took a step forward. Suddenly, he tripped over a submerged tree root, making the bottle in his hand flip into the air. Although he was still standing, he looked too frightened to go after the bottle.

I wasn't such a terrific catcher, but as I let out my two cupped hands, it fell safely into them. At the very moment it touched my bare skin, I felt a sting of pain, as if touching a flame. *"Errr!"* I groaned quietly, my head hung to my chest. After a moment, the pain was gone. *"Ahhh!"* I let out a high-pitched scream as a strong burning pain stung both my palms and fingers, resulting in hordes of blisters.

"Oh!" yelled Howie. "Put it down! Put it down! That's very powerful stuff!" I could have sworn he followed that exclamation with a snigger, but being in *so* much pain, I wasn't sure, and I didn't care for it much.

Without any hesitation, I laid it on the ground. As the grass beneath it started to smolder, Howie grabbed it with the piece of cloth. *That's what the cloth was for,* I thought to myself.

Howie took out a plastic soda bottle from his backpack, and started to pour the blood-red fluid from the glass bottle into it. While he was doing so, I studied my hands. There were huge burns and blisters all over.

As he poured the last drops of the fluid into the soda bottle, Howie asked, "Are you all right?"

"What was that?"

"It's my science experiment. It's for a school assignment."

I raised my eyebrows. "Science experiment? What's it made of? Fresh-from-Mount-Etna lava? It's rather powerful and intensely hot for a *school* science experiment." I stared at my hands again. "*And painful*," I muttered.

"*Hmmm?* Oh, right." He reached into his backpack once more, and took out a crystal-blue jar, which took the shape of an oversized diamond. There was a tiny star at the point. It was as appealing as Ryan's cauldron. Howie held it on the palm of one hand, and put his other hand on the top of the jar, screwing off the handsome lid. After lifting it by the tiny star, streams of vapors started to flow out. "Here," said Howie, holding out the opened jar, "get some of this ointment, then spread it on your hands like lotion."

I held the jar with cupped hands, careful not to drop it. A visible fountain of vapors floated out continuously, making me wonder. "This, this is no *ordinary* ointment, is it, Howie?" I asked slowly.

"*No.* No, it isn't."

"I read about this ointment in a witch doctor's book. It was, *was it . . . ?*" I tried to recall aloud. "Oh, yes, *Marvin Marsh's 'Marvelous Book of Healing for Young Witches and Warlocks.' Hmmm . . . continuous flowing of vapors . . .* oh, yes, chapter three, page three fifty-four, *Sorcerer's Choice,* instant healing ointment!" I exclaimed in delight for my sharp memory. "Is this what it is?"

"Yeah."

"I thought you couldn't do witchcraft anymore, though."

"Correct, but this is something I had made before giving up magic. Ryan must have told you about what happened to my family, huh?" he asked somberly, looking down. I nodded as I rubbed the palm of my free hand with my fingers, trying to soothe my sores and blisters. He looked at my hand, then to me, "Well, you can't just stand here all day; we'll be late for school. Just spread two fingers' worth of it on your hands."

Once I dipped my fingers in, I felt a chill of icy menthol creep up my hand like creeping fig crawls on walls. It was just like that, only it came up in a rush as if it were a raging rapid. It wasn't pasty like any ordinary ointment, although it appeared that way. Instead, it was like dipping my hands into the freezing waters of the Atlantic.

I scooped my fingers out, handed the jar back to Howie, and began to rub my hands together thoroughly. As I did so, I felt a powerful freezing sensation. It was cool, kind of like the feeling in your lungs and nasal area when you inhale the taste of a piece of winter-fresh flavored gum.

After doing this, I felt the pain of the burns and blisters go away. Seconds later, I studied my hands. There wasn't a trace of injury at all. Not only were the blisters and sores gone, but my hands were left smooth and silky.

"Gee, *thanks,* Howie!" I thanked him in complete awe.

"Oh, you're welcome," he replied as he picked up the soda bottle. Surprisingly the red liquid changed to a dark brown color, like Coke.

"Let's just keep this accident between the two of us, 'kay?"

"Sure," I said absentmindedly. "Hey, your science experiment, it's burning hot, and it *changed color.* What's it *really* made of?"

"Ah, that I cannot reveal to you."

"*Oh,* why not?"

"That's only between Mister Shnrub and me. Surely *you'd* understand?"

"Oh, yes. Of course, entirely," I replied briskly. I looked at my watch. It was still on my wrist from the other night. "We must head for school. The bell will ring in fifteen min—"

I suddenly silenced, seeing that I had been talking to myself. Howie had suddenly vanished.

I walked to school, dazed. Howie, his fire-hot, color-changing science experiment, his sudden disappearance, this was odd. Yet again, ever since my entire *normal* life has hit a climax, everything from my lifestyle to my schooling has been peculiar, and almost *eerie.* This kept me wondering all the way to school. Although deep in thought, I did not trip nor crash into anything.

It wasn't until the first ring of the "cathedral" bell, that I realized I had arrived at school. In the crowd of dull, almost lifeless teens, I spotted Phanny, Karen, and Ryan. I guessed that they spotted me first, because they were already heading my way. This worried me, because Howie told me not to tell anyone about the incident that occurred not too long ago. But because I had these thoughts glued into my head, and the fact that the three of them were telepathic, I didn't know what to do.

"What's up?" asked Phanny as they approached. The way my facial expression was, I figured that she was reading my mind. *Think of something else,* I told myself. "Is there something wrong?" She looked at me square in the eyes.

Although I had already seen Ryan, I made myself think gravely, *"Ryan's dead, and it's all my fault!"* Through the corner of my eye, I saw that Ryan *wasn't* there anymore. *Where was Ryan?*

Phanny smiled. "Hey girl, Ryan's not dead . . . *yet.*"

"What's that s'posed to mean?"

Karen answered me instead of Phanny. *"Well,* Ryan isn't as clever and defensive against dark magic as he said he was. His personality when it comes to things like that is as cowardly as much as the fact that he looks like a girl. He's—" Phanny suddenly cut in, "What she *means* is Ryan's a wuss!" She let out a quiet chuckle.

"But he didn't seem so afraid when finding out that Jenny and her coven are planning to kill him."

"Yeah," agreed Phanny, still smiling, "but in his mind he was probably going *'Oh, no! That coven of Jenny's is trying to kill me! What am I going to do? I'm such a wuss! Mommy, gimme my teddy bear!'* " She and Karen practically burst their lungs out, laughing in such uncontrollable laughter. Tears started rolling down their cheeks.

"Hey!" I yelled, as if I were the one offended. "He's probably got guts. There just hasn't been any, well, a *moment* to show it."

"Yeah, maybe," said Phanny, a little calmer. "Maybe we should dissect him when Jenny's through with him." She and Karen erupted with another roar of laughter.

"Phanny! Have my words gone through one ear and out the other?"

She looked at me as she'd just started listening to me. "What did you say?"

"Phanny!" She started to laugh.

"Now, now," Karen said, "quit playing games with her. Sure, Ryan doesn't look heroic, but the girl—" she stopped abruptly, seeing the frown forming on my face. "*Guy.* The guy might have courage somewhere within him. I guess he'll stay alive, even with Jenny and her coven, along with Tay after him."

"Thank you," I said calmly. "But then, if Ryan isn't dead, where is he?"

"I dunno; he just disappeared a while ago," answered Phanny.

"Do you know where he might have gone off to?"

She shrugged, "Not a clue."

"Hello," said a dull voice. "Did I miss anything?"

"Not really," answered Phanny, smiling.

"Where *were* you?" I asked.

He just continued to talk like when I asked him on the first day of school. Why *did* he suddenly disappear? Why did he not answer me when I asked him where he had been?

"We're going to be late," he said.

"Where were you?" I asked him, sounding more demanding this time.

"We're going to be late," he repeated.

I looked around, he was right. There was no one around but us. When I checked my watch, I realized that we had less than a three minutes to get to class. No, no, no, **HA,** let me rephrase that. *I* had less than three minutes to get to class. Just like Howie, the three of them were out of my sight in a flash. Great, ditched by my own *friends.*

I exploded through the double-doors. *Two minutes.* Down the long hallway to the left I glided. *One minute.* Halfway to room one-fifteen. *Thirty seconds.* All of a sudden, I tripped, getting the wind knocked out of me. *No,* I thought. *It can't be, not now! Twenty seconds.* It took me ten seconds to get up. *Nine . . . eight . . . seven . . . six . . .*

slip! The floor was wet. I couldn't get up. I fell on my back, hurting my tailbone. *Two . . . one . . . Bong! Bong! Bong! Bong!* The tardy bell clamored.

No! My heart sank, as I thought of the embarrassment that Madame Savant would give me as she scolded me.

I struggled to get up, taking more than five minutes. Carefully, I inched towards the door. It ached to stay standing, let alone walk. Every step I took was agony! I could tell you that it was a terribly painful, sore, agonizing, backbreaking, whatever-you-want-to-describe-the-word-*ouch*-as feeling. When I got to the door, I stretched my hands out to my sides, wiggling my fingers nervously with uneasy thoughts. Shutting my eyes tightly, I opened the door. At first, I expected to hear a *"Mees Romero! You're late! I weel have to call your parents!"* If she did, what would I tell them? What *could* I tell them? I left the house earlier in the morning. *That's ridiculous!* I told myself. *Why would she call home for just five minutes of tardiness?* I kept my eyes tightly shut.

I walked through the door, full of these thoughts. A second passed . . . ten seconds . . . half a minute . . . nothing happened. Once I took a peek of the classroom, I turned my eyes to stunned.

Madame Savant was on her way to her desk. Some of the class was standing up, facing their friends. Others were already seated, facing anywhere but forward.

It sounds normal to you, *doesn't it?* That's because you didn't see what I saw. The way I described their positions is not enough. Not only was the teacher on her way to her desk, nor was the class just not facing the front, they were also *still*. Still as in *frozen*.

Savant had her left foot off the floor, as if she were frozen before taking another step. There were smiles and gapped mouths on the teenage students, who were frozen while socializing. *Smiles?* That's odd. When I had first got there, these students had not the faintest fraction of a grin.

I walked to a corner where Karen, Phanny, and Ryan were smiling rare smiles. Glaring at them in disgust, I muttered, "Some friends you are!" I raised my voice slightly. "Leave me to be late, would you? You rot, you three—you three—**YOU THREE BAGS OF TRASH!!!** I hate you! I hope you all rot in Hell!"

Purposely, without guilt or fault, I knocked Ryan to the floor. "**YOU!**" I screamed at the lifeless mannequin. "It's *your* fault I'm late! I wouldn't have wasted time this morning conversing with Karen and Phanny if we'd never met! I would not have tried joining this stupid coven of yours!" With tremendous strength, I kicked his leg, despite my hurt tailbone. I thought I heard one of his bones crack, but at the moment I did not care. "You idiot! Why should I try saving *you?* Save yourself! Maybe if Jenny captured me, you guys would leave me alone to **DIE!**"

My whole body trembled with rage, and I was panting, furiously. I glared at them once more, and hissed, "You three are sorry excuses for friends!"

To my surprise, the three of them made one quick blink. I stepped back, as the entire class sprung back to life. They didn't seem bewildered or puzzled about anything. Everyone just continued what they were doing moments ago. Ryan, on the other hand, was on the floor, clutching his hurt, probably *broken* leg, looking very confused.

"I don't get it," said Phanny over Ryan's groans. She had her hand on her hip, scratching her head with the other. "One second we're talking about Ryan's embarrassing moments, and the next thing you know, he's down on the floor, blubbering like a baby. It's wonderful!"

"Why am I on the floor?" he groaned in a hoarse voice. *"And why does my leg feel as if it were broken?"*

He looked at me, almost in a pleading manner. I just stood there with my arms crossed, giving him a pitiless smile, watching him as he suffered. *Maybe I did break a bone or two.*

Being a big jerk, I taunted *"Aw, is ity bity Wyan huht?"* I frowned. "**Good!**"

They stared at me with puzzled frowns. I looked away, and the bell rang. Savant had just taken her seat.

"Time flies queeckly, no?" She sighed, resting her elbow on her desk.

This entire morning was odd. Everybody was frozen, as if someone, or some*thing* had stopped time. That couldn't be true, though, because my watch kept ticking the entire time.

I wanted to tell the three about this, but I doubted that they would want to hear from me, not with the way I acted. As I walked over to my first period class, I felt a stomach-churning rush of guilt surge through me like an electrical shock. I regretted what I had just done.

Thirteen
Regretful

It had been a freakish morning, but that's not what I was pondering on at all. I thought about what I did to Ryan. Although I knew that he couldn't hear me while he was frozen, I felt all my guilt *laugh* at me, putting me down.

I gazed out the window beside me during math class, resting my head on my hand. The piercing sound of the chalk being pressed against the board did not bother me at the time. In fact, I didn't pay attention to anything of my surroundings. I just gazed out the window, my mind anywhere but earth.

"Miss Romero?" A deep voice was calling my attention. "Miss Romero? **MISS ROMERO WILL YOU PAY ATTENTION?!**"

"Ohwa?" I replied dumbly. I blinked once, than three more times. "Ohwa?" I gave another dumb reply.

"*Errr!*" growled Mister Cross irritated. He wiped his forehead down to his chin. He started to cajole me through gritted teeth, "*Miss Romero, this isn't the time to daydream. In Miss Nightingale's class, you'd have an excuse, but this is my class, and you* **DON'T HAVE AN EXCUSE!**"

"Ohwa?" I still did not know what was going on.

"*Errr!* Detention! After school! Do *not* be late!" He started writing something down on a piece of red paper.

When he had slapped it onto my desk, my mind was plunged back to earth.

With a panicked voice, I exclaimed, "Detention?! But—but Mister Cross! I—but—Ryan—"

"*And what does Mister Nakano have to do with this?*"

Of course, the math teacher wouldn't be aware of the "Jenny, Ryan Dilemma." I just bowed and answered, "Nothing, sir, nothing."

He looked at me suspiciously, then continued on with his lesson. "Okay, class, as I was saying, the formula for finding the circumference of a circle is quite simple. All you have to do . . ."

I looked to the right to see Howie staring at me. He quickly turned away. As I fiddled around with the piece of paper in my hands, I remembered that I was assigned to detention. Bored, I decided to read the slip. It read:

Dark Falls Junior High
Detention Slip
**Detention Hall, Room 101
Mr. Boiler**

**I have sent my student here today because:
She refused to pay attention in class.**

I stopped reading for a moment. *I did not refuse to pay attention! What a liar!* Not wanting to get into deeper trouble, I did not argue. Instead, I continued reading.

I want his/her punishment to be:

A full review on today's math lesson

Thank you for your time,

Chris Cross
(Mr. Chris Cross)

What?! Another hour of math? I fingered the slip, checking to see if it was real. Knowing that it was very genuine, I became thunderstruck. I faced my right again. When I saw Howie facing me again, he suddenly faced forward. *That guy's weirding me out,* I thought to myself.

Suddenly, he raised his hand.

"Yes?" the teacher responded.

"Sir, is it possible if I could, um, have a quick chat with you, out in the hall?"

He looked at his watch, then sighed, "As you wish. Class, just copy down the problems on the board, then evaluate them while I talk to Mister Blanks."

Howie got off his seat, and the two of them stepped out of the classroom. I strained my ears to listen to their conversation, curious. At first, I could only hear faint whispers. All of a sudden, I heard a muffled cry for help, one of a man of deep voice. *Mister Cross!*

What was Howie *doing* to him? *Was* Howie doing something to him? Too afraid to think about the subject any further, I turned around, facing the back, and saw Phanny glaring at me. Our eyes met, her cold eyes stabbed mine. It was frightening, yet I dared not turn away. Instead, I continued to stare into the eyes of pure hatred.

For some reason, I knew that she was reading my mind. What did she want? Knowing that she could read my mind, I asked her something, using my mind to communicate.

"*What do you want?*"

Suddenly, in a matter of a split second, I felt a power that no other power could relate to. It was indescribable. I felt pressure in my brain, like a tsunami crashing against the face of a cliff.

She blinked, then, all of a sudden, I heard her answer telepathically, *"Me? I want to know why you hurt Ryan. Why do you suddenly hate the three of us?"*

"I wouldn't say hate, I was just a little ticked off, that's all. And since when did you care about Ryan? I thought you didn't like him."

"Enough talk about him! I want to know why you feel so guilty. What did you do?"

"I—I really don't want to—to talk about it."

"Come on. I'm itching to know!"

"Well, all right." As I started to talk about what I did, the whole room started to blur, and the two of us were back in homeroom . . . *"The bell rung once I touched the door knob. I was both angry, and panicked . . ."*

I talked telepathically for five minutes, until I had concluded my odd story. She looked at me, her eyes filled with guilt and solemn apology. For a few seconds, she just stared at me, being very motionless, although we really didn't have to face each other, seeing that we were conversing telepathically.

I'm talking telepathically? How did this happen? I could not recall having any history of sudden telepathic connections like this.

"Phanny, how did I start communicating telepathically?!"

"Everybody has psychic powers. They just don't know how to use them. You are one of the few who figured out how to use one of them."

"But I just sat there, talking to you through my mind."

"Exactly!"

"What?"

"Exactly!"

"I heard what you said the first time, I was just, surprised. I mean, I talk through my mind a lot of times."

"Yes, but you knew very well that I was trying to read your mind, right?"

"Yeah."

"You were communicating directly to me through your mind, knowing that I would receive the message."

"Continue."

"Well, it's difficult to explain, but, did you, by any chance, feel some kind of powerful pressure in your head? When you asked me your first question?"

"Uh huh."

"Well, that's all I could explain, it's almost unexplainable. It's like, if you try doing something that you're one-hundred percent sure would work, the power would just . . . activate."

Janice Stone, a blonde who sat next to Phanny, butted through our telepathic conversation. She too, was telepathic. She said aloud in an irritated voice, "You two'd better cut this conversation short, 'cause you might get caught. And be considerate to the other people who are telepathic, huh? We don't want to hear such conversations, *okay?*"

"Janice," came in Jake Stone, her twin brother, who sat right in front of me, "if you don't want to get tangled up in these, what you call, *boring* telepathic socials, *don't read other people's minds!*"

Jake always wanted to be in the know. He read everybody's mind now and then. A cute eavesdropper I thought he was. His eyes were a deep blue, so deep, you could fall into them forever, and he had "dirty" blonde hair that was just long enough to keep behind his ears. On each cheek was an adorable dimple. Although he had a breath-taking appearance, I had no affection towards him. Well, maybe as a *friend*.

Suddenly, the door opened. Howie walked in, but Mister Cross was nowhere to be seen. He took his seat, smiling evilly. His smile somehow frightened me. Maybe it was the thought that he might have done something *gruesome* to the man.

"*Howie,*" I said almost in a whisper, a little afraid of him, "*where is—*" Hearing footsteps nearing the class room, I did not bother to finish. Mister Cross entered the room, looking quite normal.

He walked over to his desk. Before he could take his seat, however, he called me over with his deep, aristocratic voice, "Allis—I mean, Miss Romero, could I have a word with you for a moment?"

I didn't reply, I just slowly walked towards the front. *Was I in trouble again?* When I reached the front, I swallowed hard. He pulled a stool from under his desk and patted it: a gesture telling me to sit down. My fear lessened when I saw a pleasant smile on his face, something extremely rare.

"Please take a seat, don't worry, you're not in any trouble," he talked quietly.

I sat down and looked at him, a bit puzzled. Getting very anxious, I spoke up, "What is it, sir?"

"I was wrongfully mistaken to give you detention. I clearly understand now that you probably have a lot of things on your mind. I too was once like that, back in the days of the dinosaurs."

I could hear Howie chuckling. Howie had his reasons. I mean, it didn't even sound like the serious math teacher who gave me detention. Yet, if he *was* just acting in the spirit of play, I did not see a look of a joker on his face, and what kind of person would say that they were actually from the Jurassic period and not be joking?

"May I have your detention slip?" he asked.

"Um, sure," I took out the red slip from my pocket and handed it to him.

"Thank you." He then started to do the one thing I would have least expected him to do: he started to tear the slip into tiny pieces. "Well, that's that," he carelessly said, as he sprinkled what was once my reason for anger into the wastebasket. "You may take your seat now."

I was filled with a surge of both shock and gladness. Come on, getting out of undeserved detention just by doing nothing? Really, I didn't feel much like thinking about it. I was just, too happy!

All through the day, I was itching to have gym. I wanted dearly to prevent Jenny from initiating her *evil* scheme. My mind was too anxious to notice Mister Boris's scratchy voice, or to daydream, sleepily in Miss Nightingale's class. Not even the accidental explosion in Mister Shnrub's science class made me stop thinking, although I *did* hear it. He started yelling for help with his kazoo-like voice. Neither did *that* amusing moment make me stop worrying for the slightest moment.

Suddenly, the bell rang. I ran past the teacher, who was struggling to extinguish an ignited desk. I thought I heard his kazoo-like voice say, "Goh ahead, turn yo bahck on old Meesta Shnrub!"

"Sorry, Mister Shnrub! Gotta get to class!" I yelled, really wanting to help him. *But I've got to save Ryan first!* I said to myself.

I ran down the halls and up the stairs to the gymnasium. Not wanting to make a fool out of myself by bursting into the gym, I made a sudden halt at the door.

Slowly, I opened it. Nobody was there. Checking my watch, I saw that I was seven minutes early.

I slowly walked through when I heard faint whispers. The whispers led me to the girls' locker room. Wanting to know who was there, I pressed my ear against the door.

". . . Okay, now that you're all here, let's make sure that we all know what to do. Krystine, here, keep the potion in your backpack."

"Yeah, okay," she answered.

"Katrina, use your telekinesis to get it, along with a water bottle when I freeze time, okay?"

"Okay."

Freeze?! Did she say *freeze?* Was she the one who froze everyone this morning? I listened with excitement.

"All right, so when you get it, add a generous amount into the water bottle. Krystine, so you don't have to go into the filthy boys' locker room, use *your* telekinetic powers to place the water bottle in Ryanna's backpack."

"Got it."

"And, Tay, you'll keep a close eye on him, and make sure he doesn't take a single sip of liquid throughout P.E. Notify me if he attempts to drink from the fountain. You know, so we can be sure he'll be thirsty enough to drink the poisoned water."

"Why can't I do something a bit more challenging?"

"Because," said Jenny, "I want to make sure that this would be the easiest, quickest plan as possible."

Katrina slightly frowned. "Since we're covering all the work, where do you take part in this plan of *yours?*"

"Dearest Katrina," she said calmly, "the three of you are not covering *all* the work. You forgot about the reason why he'll not even bother to think how the bottle of water got into his pack. *I'm* going to distract him from drinking anything."

"*Oh . . .*" they all said, thinking this wasn't even much.

"*Yes.* Also, I *am* the one who planned this whole thing out, right?"

"Well, yes."

"Oh, right."

"Yeah."

The three girls replied at the same time.

"Okay. Now, since we all know what to do, let's just wait out on the stairs. We've still got five minutes."

Before they could head for the door, I quickly opened the equipment closet, which was beside me, and got in. Just as the doorknob twisted, I closed the door, then opened it slightly, deciding to leave an unnoticeable gap. The locker room door was swung open, and the four of them walked out. I stepped out of the closet once I heard them exit the gymnasium. Pressing my ears against the gymnasium door, I discovered that they were walking down the steps, their voices fading away as they left.

Relieved, I gladly went out of the gym and waited out in the hall.

Fourteen
Gym-Nausea

The time between those five minutes ticked as slowly as honey dripping thickly out of a jar. At the last minute, a herd of students stampeded up the stairs and packed the doorway. When the bell rang, they somehow got through, me following. By the time I entered the locker room, everyone was in his or her gym uniform. I quickly changed as they went out the door.

After changing, I went out into the gym, finding that the three long benches that were against the walls were already occupied. I joined Phanny, Karen, and Ryan, who were kneeling on the matted floor. Once I sat on the mat, I started to warn Ryan about Jenny's plan, wanting to make sure he wouldn't drink the poisoned bottle of water.

"Ryan," I started uneasily, facing them, "guys, um, I was being a little nosy, and I just wanted to warn you. You see—" I suddenly stopped when the gymnasium door flung open.

Miss Felton appeared at the doorway in her gym uniform, a silver whistle dangling from her neck. Everyone fell silent and watched her. She walked over to the equipment closet and opened it. Bending down, she took out two basketballs. From her shorts pocket, she took out a remote control.

Before shutting the closet door, she pointed the control at the empty rectangular spot at the corner of the gym and pressed a button. Something happened when she did that, something I thought no school gym was activated to do. The flooring, to that once empty spot, literally flipped over, revealing a basketball court. It was so awesome! I've never *dreamed* that *any* kind of school would have such a thing. As usual, no one but me showed any interest.

Suddenly, Miss Felton blew on the whistle, which made an awful screech. I faced her. "Fall in line!" she called out in her tough voice. Everyone scrambled off the benches and rapidly formed two straight lines. "We've been—"

"**OW!!!**" screamed Jenny falsely. "Ally-rat Romero kicked me!"

My eyes widened in disbelief and anger. I was right next to her, so it was believable, but believe me, she was being a big, fat, *liar!* And *Ally-rat Romero?!* The nerve! I looked at her with my mouth wide open. "*No I didn't!*"

"Yes, you did. I saw you!" she said quickly and airily.

"**NOW, LADIES!!!**" boomed the teacher. We stopped dead. "What the bloody blazes is going on here!"

"Well—" I started to say.

"Oh, Miss, she kicked me!" said Jenny quickly in one of those so-fake *I'm-a-hurt-little-rich-girl-help-me tones.*

"*I did not!*"

"Yes, you did!"

"Oh, great, you're a snob *and* a liar!"

"*Uh!* Watch it, *Ally-rat,* or I'm going to—"

"*The name's Allison you, b—*"

"**DO I HAVE TO SEND YOU TO MISTER KAEHLER'S OFFICE?!**"

We glared at each other, then shook our heads.

The teacher eyed us for a moment, then continued.

"As I was saying, we've been doing gymnastics for quite a while now. I just thought we could start something new today."

I kicked Jenny for real. She winced, glared at me, and put me in a mind grasp. I groaned.

The teacher didn't notice. She just dribbled the two balls simultaneously at a high rate, then spun the right one on her fingertip, still dribbling the other one. Without warning, she threw the one right at Howie, who was the first one of the line nearest to the teacher. It smacked him right on the nose, making an awful *crack!* Blood started to trickle from his nose to his chin.

Jenny and I stopped, stunned.

"Not fast enough, are you, *Mister Blanks?*" remarked the teacher, smiling as if she had told a smart joke. "Go to the nurse and ask her to give you some wound-mending potion. Bitter potion, but it works. Heard Mister Nakano just got his *mysteriously* broken leg mended a few hours ago."

Howie ran out the door, which was still opened. His hands were cupped around his bloody nose.

"Tell her to give you a quicker eye too!" she called mockingly after him. She faced us once more and clapped her hands once. "Okay, give me the ball." Once she was handed the ball, she started to spin it again, everyone now aware that it could be swatted at any one of them.

All of a sudden, she made a move so inhumanly quick that Tay was already holding the ball. I didn't even see what happened.

"Excellent catch, Tay!" praised Miss Felton, giving her a thumbs-up. That's when I realized that that she had thrown the ball at Tay in a flash. Tay was some catcher! "Tay, pick out nine other people, and separate five of them to form a competing team. Then, assign them a captain."

"Okay."

After she picked Jake Stone to be the other team's captain, Howie dropped in, literally! He came from a hidden door from the ceiling.

"Hello, *Blanks,*" said the teacher bitterly, "nice of the nurse to *drop* you over to class."

"Miss Felton," called Tay, smiling, "could I dismiss Jake from that team and replace him with *Howie?*" Miss Felton answered with a wicked smile, then nodded.

The other team groaned. Jake shrugged and let Howie get off the floor to replace him. For forty minutes, we played basketball, at least, that's what I thought. When I saw the students looking at me, I was plunged out of my sea of thoughts.

"Allison, you've been hit by the ball at least a few dozen times," said Jake. "What's up with that?"

"I dunno," I said half obliviously.

"Okay, time to change, people! See you all on Monday!" yelled Miss Felton. "Oh, yes, Blanks' team, you did great!"

They frowned harder and started muttering at Howie. "You big loser! What a disgrace!" I heard someone say. It *was* somewhat true, since his team lost fifty seven to zip.

I quickly changed and burst out of the locker room, hoping that nothing had happened to Ryan yet. Unfortunately, I came out to see a crowd around Ryan, who had become violently ill. He stopped, put a hand on his forehead, looking extremely dizzy, then continued to vomit. When he had finished, he groaned, then finally, collapsed.

Fifteen
The Stick and the Stone

The paramedics arrived, and Ryan was rushed to the hospital. I watched as the ambulance drove away, feeling at fault. This, I thought, *was all my fault.* It was my fault for not being attentive enough during that whole time. It was my fault that Jenny was succeeding.

Since school was already over, I went home. This time, I did not walk home tangled in my thoughts, or enjoying the beauty of the woods. No. I just walked, blank of thoughts, not taking pleasure in nature's art.

I unlocked the front door to my house, not calling out to my parents as I usually did. As I climbed up the stairs hunch-backed, I came across a thought. *Jenny, Krystine, Katrina, and Tay were still in the locker room while Ryan was being ill. It would have been impossible for Jenny to have frozen us without us knowing—*

I stopped my reasoning, remembering this morning's awkward moment in homeroom. No one noticed that they were frozen. We could have been frozen during gym and not have noticed it.

Ryan could have seen that bottle of water in his backpack while he was in the locker room and gratefully gulped it down. After that, he probably walked out and got sick right on the spot. This was a logical reason for Ryan's sudden illness.

Yet again, I didn't ask him anything about him drinking it yet. I could just see him at the hospital and ask him if he drank, ate, or did anything right before he started feeling nauseated. There was no debate. I decided to go to the hospital to question him.

I went to the family room to ask my dad if he could drive me to the hospital. Instead of seeing my dad reading a newspaper on his comfy recliner, I saw my mom, asleep in her rocker.

"Mom," I whispered into her ear. "Mom, wake up."

"Those are nice trunks you have on, Gregoreo," she murmured, dreamily.

"Mom!" I shook her slightly.

"Huh?" She woke up with a start. "Oh, yeah. Um, what is it?" She straightened herself and looked at me.

"Where's Dad? I want to go to the hospital. Ryan's there. Got sick after P.E."

"Oh, I'm sorry. Your father went to a job orientation at the science lab. He's over there at the Dark Falls Science Institution building not too far from here. But I'm sure he'll be—who's at the hospital?"

"Ryan."

"Your friend?"

I muttered, "No, not really."

"What?"

"I said, yeah, really."

"Well then, if you want, we could drive there. Some people from the lab picked up Daddy. So we have the van all to ourselves."

"Sure. Thanks, Mom,"

We drove only a mile and a half down the road right from our house—which is where I was heading on my first day at Dark Falls Junior High. The Tuyen Lee Hospital was five dozen times the size of the middle school. My mom parked in a parking lot that could have been another neighborhood. After easily finding a parking space, we walked to the main entrance.

My mom and I walked over to the nurses' station. "Excuse me," said my mom, "where can we locate Ryan Nakano?"

"Relations?" asked a wizened nurse with a sour voice and a New Yorker accent.

"Friends," I informed.

"Okay. Room 344, third floor. You've got an hour." To me, she sounded very un-nurse-like.

"Thank you," said my mom politely.

When we entered an elevator, I pressed the button that had a *3* on it, and up we went. *Ting!* There was a tiny bell sound, and the doors slid open. Right in front of us was the door to room 344. I opened the door, and my heart sank. A nurse covered a dead body with a white sheet.

"Ryan's *dead?!*" I shrieked frantically.

"Yes, I'm sorry," said the kind-voiced woman. "He just never clothed himself. Went everywhere unclothed, the nut!"

"What was his illness?" asked my mom.

"Hypothermia. Had it since this morning while standing outside bare-naked from dawn."

"WHAT?!" I exclaimed. "No, no, no. He was just sent here *after school!*"

Her face brightened up, and she said smiling, "Oh, you must be looking for Ryan *Nakano,* right?"

I nodded.

"Well then, that's room 434."

My mom and I sighed in relief. There was silence in the room for a short while.

"If that's where he is," my mom broke the ice, "then who's this?"

"Huh?" the nurse turned around and looked as if she had just noticed the corpse lying on the bed. "Oh, this is Ryan Naked-go, a.k.a. Ryan Noble. I guess Nurse Mona directed you. You know, the New Yorker with the sour voice?"

"Yeah."

She shook her head slowly, clicking her tongue. "Poor Mona," she said in a sorry voice. "Thinking she's still a nurse. She never did get out of rehab. You see, she's in rehab, trying to snap out of the fact that she was fired from this hospital years ago. Crosses from the rehabilitation building next to the ER all the time to come 'play nurse.' Tons of visitors get lost because of her. It was on my third week here . . ."

She continued on as I said, "Yeah, um, we have to–go–now. Uh, huh. Ya, thanks. Bub-bye. *Hee!*"

We shut the door and went back into the elevator. Once we arrived on the fourth floor, we searched for room four thirty-four. It was farther away than we had expected. We went up and down corridors, and twisted through hallway after hallway.

When we finally reached what we hoped was the correct room, I tapped on the door. A short and stout woman peered from behind. "Are you here to see Ryan Nakano?"

"Yes," answered the two of us.

She sighed. "Okay, come in."

The nurse opened the door and let us enter. There were four sheet-drawn cubicles. She led us to the one on the far left. The three of us entered the cubicle and walked towards Ryan, who was lying on the bed, watching as we approached. I laid my hands on the safety bar of the bed. As I saw his weak face, it hurt inside to think about what I did to him that morning.

"Hey!" he said hoarsely yet delighted to see us. He gave me a weak smile. "What are you doing here?"

"I came here to visit you." I looked around and started to talk telepathically. *"I need to ask you some questions. Do you have a plan on getting the two of them out for a moment?"*

"Since when?" he said aloud, still very hoarse.

"Shhh!" I put my finger on my lips.

"Oh, right." He was the talking telepathically. *"Okay, ask your mom for hot cocoa. Tell her it's downstairs, near the nurses' station."*

"And Nurse Tea Pot?"

"I'll take care of her."

"Okay."

I spoke aloud, "Mom, could you fetch me a cup of cocoa please? They're near the nurses' station."

"Well, now that you mention it, I *do* need a warm drink. . . . Okay, I'll get some. Just wait here, I'll be right back."

"Nurse?" Ryan groaned. "I'm feeling nauseous. Could I have some medicine?"

"Oh! All right! I'll be back, just hold it, hold it!" She nervously ran out the door after my mom.

I gave him a five. "Smooth move, Bro!"

"Thanks," he croaked. "Now what was it you needed to ask me?"

"Oh, yeah. When did you, you know, get nauseous?"

"After I drank a bottle of soda that Jake gave me in the locker room after P.E. Said it was from Miss Felton."

"Jake *Stone?*"

"Yeah."

"He can't be a suspect! He wouldn't dare!"

"You're looking for suspects?"

"*Duh!*"

"Jake isn't exactly the one to blame. Maybe it was Felton, that stick of a P.E. teacher. I mean, Jake *did* say it was from her."

He stared at the ceiling for a moment. "You know," he said finally, "she could have been the one who killed Howie's family."

"Where're you getting that?"

"Well, last year, when he and I entered middle school, he'd pass Miss Felton on his way to the sixth-grade gym, it's the door before the seventh-grade gym, you see. I'd usually walk with him, and every time we passed that stick, she'd say 'Miss your family yet, Blanks?' "

"That's a possibility," I mused. "But all I'm trying to focus on right now is this: who's behind what just happened to you today? For all we know, they could be space aliens trying to kill you!"

He gave a hoarse laugh. "What for? I don't hold the world together or anything."

"Maybe it was Jenny."

"Jenny?"

"Yeah. Maybe she gave it to Jake and said it was from Miss Felton."

I told him about what I found out about Jenny, how I broke my promise to him by spying on Jenny.

"So that's why you were hit by the basketball dozens of times at P.E. and never noticed it," said Ryan, not angry at the fact that I broke a promise.

"I was worried," I replied quietly. "I can't bear to lose a friend."

"You're a loyal friend, Allison," said Ryan warmly.

We heard footsteps drawing nearer and nearer. "Let's talk on Monday. I'll be well by then."

" 'Kay."

My mom and the pudgy nurse came in.

"Here's your hot cocoa," said my mom, handing me a steaming styrofoam cup of cocoa.

"Thanks," I replied, taking the cup, and sipping from it.

"Um, Nurse," I heard Ryan croak, "I feel better now. I don't think I would be needing the medicine anymore."

"Oh, is that what you needed? I thought you said you wanted some cinnamon."

"That'll do." Ryan smiled.

After finishing our hot cocoas, my mom and I said good-bye to Ryan and left for home.

Sixteen
The Mandate of Hecate

It was Saturday, and Ryan was at home, not too well. I needed to tell him and the others about yesterday's uncanny morning, most especially about Howie. His science experiment that burned; what was it? Also that *ring* . . . the ring! That was the most odd thing. The glass pupil showed that there was power in its midst. It was no ordinary ring, not at all.

I sat up on my bed, staring blankly at the door. Suddenly, someone knocked from behind. "Ally, are you awake? Phanny and Karen are here to see you." My mom was calling me.

"What?" I yelled, bursting out of the sleeping bag. *I was in my pajamas!* "Oh, wait! Just a second!" I quickly changed into my new *style:* a black tank top, and a black pair of jeans. Of course I couldn't forget the usual ponytail. "Okay, come in." I opened the door.

"Hey, Ally!" Phanny smiled.

"What are you doing here?" I asked, a little worn out from changing so quickly.

Karen leaned against me and whispered into my ear, "We sensed something was wrong."

"Well," said my mom, "I'll leave you three to yourselves." She walked out the door, and we heard her go down the stairs.

Phanny came up to me. "*Is* there something bothering you?"

"Well, kind of," I said, a little hesitantly.

"Kind of?" asked Karen, "It doesn't sound like it."

"I guess you're right."

Phanny asked comfortingly, "Was it about yesterday in homeroom? Do you think we're mad at you or something?"

"Because we're not," finished Karen.

"No. It's not that at all."

"Is it Ryan? Because he's fine. On his way to recovery, safe at home I heard. Although . . . he *is* still throwing up a lot." I saw that she held her palm-sized amethyst, as usual.

"Well . . . sort of," I replied.

"What's really biting you?" asked Phanny.

I told them about the incident when we bumped into each other and when I discovered the ring, though Howie had told me not to say a word of it. "Well, yesterday morning, I was walking to school, and I accidentally bumped into Howie. He got nervous and started to brush me off. While he was doing so, I noticed he had on a ring. It had an image of an eye on it. The pupil was made of glass and contained swirls of gray mist, and then a powerful flash of blinding light shined out from it. It actually felt like it held an extraordinary power."

Karen fiddled around with the tiny amethyst in her hand and thought for a moment. "Was the band spiral-like?"

"Yeah," I answered, a little surprised. "How did you know?"

"Hmmm . . . I have a thought. S'okay if we go and check out the library?"

"I suppose. Let me ask my parents." We all went down into the kitchen.

"Good morning!" said my parents happily.

"Is it okay if we go to the library?" I asked.

"Sure," answered my mom. "It's wonderful to read. But do you want a little something before you leave, first?"

"Uh, no thank you, Mrs. Romero. We're fine," answered Phanny.

"Are you sure?"

"Oh, yes."

"Definitely."

"Yeah." We all replied something different at the same time.

"Well, okay. Just don't stay out too late. At least come over for lunch, would you?"

"That'll be great!" we all replied cheerfully.

We arrived at the Dark Falls Local Library, located across the street from the hospital.

"Wanna see Ryan?" Phanny asked.

"I thought he was at home."

"He is. He lives a block from the hospital."

"Oh."

"So do you want to go?"

"No," I answered. "This is more important."

The two of them looked very surprised.

"What's the matter?" asked Karen. "Before, you used to care so much about every single thing that happens to him, but now, he has nausea caused by poisoned soda, and you don't give a damn about it."

I shrugged. "Are we going in or not?"

They looked at each other in shock. "Come on,

Allison!" shouted Karen. "We know something's up. Why do you seem to hate Ryan so much now?"

"Hate? No, no, no. On the contrary!" I paused. "I, I care about him more. I care about what happened to him yesterday. Last night, I went to visit him at the hospital, you know, to ask him some questions. Said the soda was from the stick, Felton, but was given by Jake Stone.

"Really, I still care." I sighed, "I guess I'm wrong about this being more important than friendship, but I feel this is important as well. Besides, Ryan'll be all right, I know he will." I paused again, then said, "So . . . are we going inside or what?"

"Let's go inside," said Phanny.

We went inside. Karen led us to the front desk of the circular library with mazelike aisles of books. There the librarian sat. She was a wizened woman wearing spectacles, who had her long gray hair tied in a neat bun. Her spectacles were a gleaming ruby-red, and a black cloak with tassels wrapped the top of her plain cotton dress—which, too, was black.

"Hello, Mrs. Willow," greeted Karen in an innocent voice.

The librarian answered in a slow, creaky voice, "Why hello, children."

"Do you know where I could find a book on Mandate Rings?"

"Why, yes! Aisle four of the sorcery section."

"Okay. Thank you."

When we got to the sorcery section, I saw the most incredible collection of books that I've ever laid eyes upon in my whole life. There were books about how to contact the dead, books of assorted potions and *Sorcerer's Choice* ointments, and spell books. There were even whole rows of books on Merlin and books of the dark arts.

"Hey, Allison," whispered Phanny. "Wanna check out this shelf?" She pointed at a shelf that was labeled:

DEATH CURSE VICTIMS AND THEIR FAMILIES

"Why would I be interested?" I asked puzzled.

"Howie's in a ton of these books, see. There's a whole bunch of books, most based on the *Heinous Death Curse of '98.*" She pointed at a section of the shelf that had at least a couple of dozen books with Howie's sulky face on the cover.

"*Hmmm,*" I was very interested. "Maybe later. I'm very curious about the ring still."

"Hey, where's Karen?" Phanny said, turning around.

The two of us poked our heads from behind the shelf.

There, was Karen, who was already sitting at a table, a tower of books kept her head from view. We walked over to her, relieved that she already covered the work of searching. I picked up the top book, "*The Mandate of Hecate?* What's all this for?"

"That ring," said Karen, her nose buried in *A Guide to Conjuring Mandate Rings for Dummies,* "is a mandate ring."

"A mandate ring? What's that?"

Karen looked up from the book and at me. "Girl, what does mandate mean?"

"Permission," I answered, without a thought.

"Right. So put the words together."

"I *know* it's a *permission ring,* but what's it used for? How does it work?"

"Depends. There are many great witches, warlocks, wizards, sorcerers, and so forth. They have many powers, and if a person of magic wants a mate, good fortune, more power, et cetera, what they need, is a mandate ring. They are rings that get you permission by Merlin to Hecate to get these things."

"Hecate? You mean the goddess who ruled magic and dark doings of night? The one from Shakespeare's *Macbeth?*"

"Yeah. It just so happens that she's a real character after all." She went back to her reading.

I looked at the cover of the book that I was holding. There were pictures of many odd-looking rings on it. As I studied the assortment of rings, all with spiral bands, I saw something that caught my eye.

"Here it is!" I exclaimed, forgetting where I was. Karen and Phanny jumped, figuratively.

"Shhh!" Karen hushed me. "What is it?"

"I found the ring that Howie was wearing," I whispered.

"Spiral band . . . of course! It's a ring of Hecate! Turn to the page that tells about the ring with the eye."

It didn't take me long till I found the page. There it was, a photo of the ring almost filled up a page, leaving space on the top for the caption, which said: *The Mandate Ring of Hecate; Power enhancement.* On the next page, was a little passage about the ring.

"Well," said Phanny anxiously, "what's it say?"

I started reading, "Hecate's power enhancement ring, is one of the most powerful of mandate rings. The glass pupil holds the power to enhance one's ability to do sorcery, wizardry, or witchcraft. One who entrusts the permission of Hecate to gain the pupil's almighty force, he or she is invulnerable, hence its name. But if the ring should fall into evil's hands, anyone involved in any kind of magic would be in grave danger."

I stopped reading. Why would Howie need such a ring? I thought he gave up doing witchcraft . . .

"Uh, Allison," Phanny started waving her hands before my face, as I thought. "Why'd you stop reading?"

"Huh? Oh, I was just wondering, why would Howie need a ring to ask for more power? I thought he quit all that magic stuff three years ago."

"Maybe he found it on the ground and wore it 'cause he thought it looked cool," joked Phanny.

I gave a small grin. "I guess you're right."

"Well then, let's just go to your place for lunch then."

"But what about the rest of this stuff on the ring?"

"Forget it," said Karen, "we found all we needed to know. The rest probably tells us how to activate the thing anyway."

"Oh, okay."

We stood up and walked away, leaving the piles of books on the table. As we walked between the bookshelves, Howie emerged from the mandate ring area.

"Ouch!" exclaimed Phanny angrily when he bumped into her. "Watch where you're going, twerp!"

"Oh, sorry, Phanny! I didn't see you!" He sounded down right scared.

"Oh, Howie. It's okay. I didn't know it was you."

His hands were folded together, shaking it as he begged for mercy. Karen saw the ring.

"*Hey,*" she said in a tone of interest, "that's a mandate ring, isn't it, Howie?"

"Er—well, I dunno. I found it on the ground in the woods. I kept it on because I thought it looked cool, don't you think?" He stuck his hand out, like a woman showing off her engagement ring.

Phanny nudged me, grinning from ear to ear. I guess she was excited that her joke of a theory was quite accurate after all.

Karen smiled and agreed, "Yeah! It looks *real cool.* Well, we have to go. See you at school Monday!"

"Bye!" we all said in a quiet chorus.

We walked out of the library and headed for my house. On the way, we kept silent, despite our findings on the ring that Howie wore. Though the confettilike leaves rained on us as the uplifting sound of pouring and splashing water filled the woods, we walked on, feeling nothing inside. We just walked on, our minds completely erased chalkboards.

Although we walked without knowing where we were going, we found ourselves at the front door of my house in no time. There I realized that I forgot to bring my house key. My thoughts felt as though they had been sucked back into my head as I knocked on the door.

"Mom, Dad! I'm home!"

"*Errr,* just a sec!" yelled my dad. He sounded as if he were stuck in something. We waited for about five minutes—though he told us it would just take a second. The door opened. There in front of us, was a monster that was six feet tall, waved many tentacles, and wore a round glass helmet.

"Aaaaaaaaaaaaaaaaaaaaaaaaaaaaaaaaaaaaaaaaaaaa aaaaaaaaaaaaaaaaaaaaaaaaaaaaaaaaaaaaaaaaaaaa aaaaaaaaaaaaaaaaaaaaaaaaaaaaaaaaaaaaaaaaaaaa aaaaaaaaaaaaaaaaaaaaaaaaaaaaaaaaaaaaaaaaaaaa aaaaaaaaaaaaaaaaaaaaaaaaaaaaaah!!!!!!!!!!" (*Deep breath*)

"Aaaaaaaaaaaaaaaaaaaaaaaaaaaaaaaaaaaaaaaaaaaa aaaaaaaaaaaaaaaaaaaaaaaaaaaaaaaaaaaaaaaaaaaa aaaaaaaah!!!!!!!!!!!!!"

The monster placed its hand on either side of its fishbowl-like helmet and pulled it off. We held our breaths. "Hiya, girls! What're you screaming about!" It was only my dad, wrapped up in electrical wires, rope, and a fishbowl.

We let go of our breaths as we laughed at our silly mistake, and at my dad's appearance. In a few minutes, we calmed down. "Dad," I questioned, still smiling, "what *happened* to you?"

He pulled off some of the wire and rope, and started, "I got in an accident down at my lab."

"Lab?" asked Phanny with great interest. "You have a lab?"

My dad nodded. "In our basement."

She looked at me with excitement. "You do?" I just shrugged. "Too cool!"

We spent a whole lunch with an endless, "Can we see the lab?" from Phanny, each followed by a, "Later," from me.

After finishing a delightful lunch of chicken adobo (chicken simmered in soy sauce and other spices) and rice, Karen spoke up, "Mister and Misses Romero, we were thinking about visiting Ryan, if that's okay with you two."

"Yeah, that's okay," answered my mom.

"Why not?" asked my dad.

I looked at Phanny and Karen, confused. No one had informed me about this visit.

"But I—"

Karen continued, drowning my words, "Would it be okay if we went right now?"

"Oh, sure. That's quite all right."

"Thank you." She and Phanny stood up, taking me by the arms. "By the way, thank you for lunch, it was terrific!"

"But I don't—"

"Shhh! C'mon!" Phanny whispered, as they dragged me out the dining room, through the hallway, then out the front door.

Seventeen
Vision in the Water

After being shoved out the door and down the driveway, I just had to know what was going on.

"What are you doing?"

"*We, are going to show you something that will blow your mind!*" replied Phanny excitedly. She had the widest smile the world has ever seen. "*But first, we have to get some supplies.*"

"*Oh Phanny, not again!*" Karen groaned. "I thought we were only *showing* her."

"What are you up to?" I asked, suspiciously.

"You'll see!" said Phanny, blissfully.

When we reached Phanny's house, 2091 Tsan Lane, she led us up a gravel driveway that led us to a garage. Phanny lifted up the door to the garage and slipped in. Before shutting the door, she turned to us.

"Aren't you two coming in?" she asked Karen and me.

"Oh, right," we both replied. We all gathered in the dark room. At first, I expected to see a dusty workbench scattered with tools, cobweb-covered corners, and a pile of junk here and there, but that's not what I saw at all.

When Phanny flicked on the lights, I saw, not a junky storage room, but a tidy, well-maintained lab. In the back, was a workbench. Instead of being littered with tools, there was a metal rack of neatly placed vials, a neat stack of tattered spell books, and jars containing mysterious herbs and liquids. On the walls, were oil painted portraits of creepy looking people. Everything was free of dust, and there wasn't a cobweb in sight. The place looked clean enough to eat off of.

I turned around. Phanny was digging into a cardboard box, taking things out and throwing them into a messy pile, while Karen watched in a disagreeing way. In the pile, I saw a crank, a harness, a witch costume, a tape recorder, and a broomstick. I picked up the pointed witch's hat.

"What's all this for?" I asked Phanny.

"I'll tell you soon," she replied absentmindedly as she browsed through the box. Suddenly, she stopped, and yanked something out of the box while excitedly yelling, "I found it! I found it!"

"Found what?" I asked, examining Phanny's clenched hand in the air.

She shook her clenched hand, "This." At that moment, I saw something transparent dangling from her hand like a rope. "Can you see it?"

"Yeah, kind of," I said squinting my eyes. "What is it?"

"An invisible rope," she proclaimed. "It's made of entwined surgical tubes."

Karen looked annoyed. "So you *are* planing to do it!" She had a slight tone of anger in her voice.

"Do what?" I was growing more anxious and very impatient.

"You'll find out when we get there," said Phanny as she stood up.

"Get where?"

"Follow us," she answered as she lifted the garage door. "Let's go."

* * *

We were walking through the woods. I was familiar with the route we were taking, because this was the path I used to enjoy tranquillity in solitude. There was a soft breeze, and the falling leaves were dancing dolls. In a few minutes, we reached the exact same waterfall and stream where I met Ryan.

"This is what you dragged me off for?" I asked a little angry. "To see the waterfall that I see nearly every day?"

"Nope!" replied Phanny, cheerfully. "It's a little *beyond* the water."

"What is that supposed to mean?"

"Stick your hand into the water," answered Karen.

"What?! Are you insane?! Ryan told me that those fish in there are carnivorous!"

"Yes," Karen nodded, "we're quite aware of what Ryan told to you, but that wasn't the *real* reason why he got you to refrain from touching the water." I looked at her in disbelief. "Go ahead, dip your hand in."

For a moment, I hesitated, then I cautiously brought my shaky hand into the water. The fish suddenly disappeared, and the water seemed to swirl. A vision came from the surface or maybe *in* the water. I yanked my hand out in a snap, shocked.

"Eeh! Wh—what was that?" I squealed.

"Calm down, girl!" Phanny laughed.

"Ha, ha, ha!" giggled Karen. "Yeah, it's only a directory."

"D-d-directory? In the—the—the w—water?"

"*Yeah!* Of Salem."

"S—S—S—*Salem?*" I was scared out of my wits. "Of Massachusetts?" They nodded. I became pale and started running about screaming and flailing my hands in the air as if they were on fire. I was in a dancing frenzy, screaming out words rapidly, "Ahhh! Salem! Where? Ahhh! Someone, anyone, get me out of here? Help! We're in Salem! Salem! Villagers! Massachusetts! Salem! Angry mob! Torches! Bad folks! Witches! Me, you, witches! Ah! Aaah! Aaaaaaah!"

"*Shhh!*" hushed Phanny, grabbing my arm and putting a hand over my mouth. "You'll attract the villagers!" She took her hand off.

"What's going on?" I asked, still scared.

"Have you ever wondered where Dark Falls is located?" asked Phanny.

"Well, *yeah.*"

She grinned, then poked her hand through the falling water. "A thin wall hides Dark Falls' real location." She took her hand out. Not a drop of water trickled down her fingers.

I looked at my own hand. Like hers, it was completely dry! "My hand," I said in a quivered whisper, "it's *dry.*"

Phanny looked at me and said quietly, "That's because it's not water. It's a gateway through the wall, hiding us from the malicious and prejudiced people of Salem."

Karen spoke up, "In 1692, as you might know, twenty people who were accused for doing witchcraft were severely tortured and prosecuted. They were put to trials, burned, strangled, needled to death, and whatnot. The witches and warlocks got so sick of it. Years later, a miracle happened.

"One day, a teen Chinese witch went deep into the woods while running away from an angry mob. She soon came out of the thick trees, to an area where the air was musty and the ground was barren and cracked. The only thing ahead of her was a high, and very steep cliff. The mob was getting closer, and she had no choice but to try and climb the cliff.

"She jumped towards the cliff, getting prepared to grasp its rough surface. Instead of hitting the hard rock, she went right through it, as if it were a hologram. Seconds later, she found herself kneeling in an artificial stream with a waterfall behind her, where she had passed through. Surrounding her, was a whole different world. A little shaken, she stuck her head through the falling water. She saw the cracked ground and the shadows of the mob emerging from the curtain of trees. Seeing this, she quickly went back in.

"She heard a man say, 'The girl flew!' They gasped and murmured. Soon, they all left out of fright. The girl stayed in there for a while and searched for inhabitants, but found none. She also found out that this place was more than hidden land. It was a whole different realm, where magic goes further than incantations and potions. People there can see the future, bewitch things, entrance people, fly, and much, much more. This directory was here since the time when it was discovered. It and everything else seemed to be enchanted. This was what amazed her even more.

"That night, she ordered an assembly for those of the 'magic society,' talking to them about her discovery. She then took them to this place. It was thence forth, called Dark Falls, because of all the *dark* memories that went on behind the waterfall."

"Wait, hold it a second," I interrupted. "We've been talking about *the girl,* and never mentioned *the girl's* name."

"Oh, yes. Her name was Tuyen Lee, a Chinese witch who was born in Salem. Tuyen grew up to be an amazing healer of this town, and a hard-working mother. In fact, the hospital's named after her. She married a man named Chang Nakano." She stopped, seeing my surprised expression, then continued, "Yes, the founder of our town is an ancestor of Ryan. He's one of her descendants."

"And we're going to scare the descendants of those witch-haters who brought her here!" said Phanny cheerfully, holding up the invisible rope. "They'll think we're actually flying!"

"I'm not in this," Karen muttered.

"We'll be back on Monday morning." Phanny waved at me, "Bye!" They both walked through the waterfall.

I stood there, awestricken for a moment. Suddenly, I felt a tap on my shoulder. I jumped with a start. "Huh?"

"So you found out about Salem and me, huh?" It was Ryan. "Unbelievable, eh?"

I didn't turn, but replied, "Yeah, kinda."

"You gotta get home. You'll miss dinner."

I turned around to find out that he was gone.

Eighteen
A Beginning to Doom

The day before was odd indeed. I still couldn't get over the fact that Dark Falls was actually located in Salem, of *Massachusetts*. Knowing my parents would question me about the shocked expression on my face, I just grabbed a muffin on my way out the door. I decided to calm my nerves by walking through the woods in the morning crisp air as I bit through a blueberry muffin.

As usual, my remedy of using water therapy for calming my nerves, worked—although the water wasn't real. Curiosity built up in my head as I approached the waterfall. *Was the vision real?* Are we really in Salem? How did we get from Los Angeles to Massachusetts in such a short period of time? Why did my dad—who is definitely not a warlock—get a job here?

I got to the waterfall, then stuck my hand in the mouth of the stream. The vision suddenly appeared. It was an awesome vision. The directory was a full map of the village itself. At the bottom, was a legend, defining what each symbol stood for. A blue dot was considered "one of us," a red dot was a villager, a rope with a head is an execution area, and if I go on, I'll never get to my point.

I looked at the edge of a large patch of green triangles, which represented the woods, where a large amount of red dots were fleeing from two blue dots, who were supposedly Karen and Phanny.

I giggled to myself. "You're doing great, guys!" There was a tap on my shoulder. I yanked my hand from the water as I gasped, losing the directory altogether.

"What are you doing?" said a familiar expressionless voice—only this time it wasn't expressionless at all! This voice had a spark of a playful, happy tone.

"Huh?" I turned around, and I saw Ryan in his black coat, as usual. Today though, his strictly neat hair was loosened up. His bangs, which were usually parted and combed to one side, were down, covering his forehead. "Oh, just wanted to see how Karen and Phanny are doing. Curious, that's all."

He knelt down and stuck his hand in the water. The directory reappeared, and he smiled, "Phanny just doesn't rest from that gimmick, does she?"

"No, she doesn't," replied a voice, not mine, though. Ryan turned around, and was facing Jenny and Krystine. In the background, were Tay and Katrina, who were restraining me with ropes. "Which is good, since there is no one to help you," finished Jenny.

"Oh, is that so?" asked Ryan calmly, as he reached into his pocket.

Krystine stared hard at the pocketed hand. Ryan groaned in pain, as she lifted his hand from the pocket with her eyes. Ryan dropped a crystal-blue potion bottle.

"*Quite so,*" Jenny grinned. She picked up the bottle. "How did you think you were going to make us drink this? By throwing it at our mouths?" She tossed the bottle as she laughed. The other three joined her, not noticing that the bottle had landed a yard from my feet. Since I was tied up, I had a reason to "accidentally" fall forward.

I effortlessly made myself fall face first. My

wrists—which were tied to the front—broke my fall. They were right on top of the bottle, which I secretively slipped into my jeans pocket.

"Get up!" shouted Jenny. I struggled to get up. She turned and looked at Krystine and Katrina. "Just take her to my basement. You too, Tay. I'll deal with her later. I've got plans for this guy."

" 'Kay," they answered.

"Hey! Watch it!" I yelled, as they nearly twisted my arms. Tay's grip hurt especially. They brought me to a mansion that was surrounded by an onyx wall, sealed with an iron gate. On either side of the gate were stone statues of gargoyles. Their eyes were sparkling rubies, which gave me chills.

Katrina muttered something and the gates slid open automatically. *Man, Jenny must be rich!* I thought to myself, as they led me up a cement path crested with an assortment of gemstones. On either side, were hedges, walling the carpet of well maintained grass, animal shaped bushes, giant golden bird cages that contained heavenly doves, and marble fountains, pouring out sparkling water.

"Yes," replied Krystine, as if I had spoken that aloud. "The Tsan Family are the billionaires of Dark Falls."

"She doesn't deserve to be in that family," I muttered to myself. I didn't know if it was what I said, but for some reason, Tay approached me with a small wooden plank, hitting it against her palm, threateningly. All of a sudden, she struck me on the back of my head. I felt the pain of my life, then, I fell to the ground, unconscious.

Nineteen
The Reverie Potion

I woke up hours later, in a cold, stony place, which was poorly lit. My vision was a little blurred, and the back of my head still ached with a sharp pain. Soon, my vision became crystal-clear, and I sat up. Though the cavernous room was large enough to keep a party of one hundred in, there was nothing but a water heater, a dangling light bulb, and cobwebs on the stony walls.

Suddenly, a giant spider crawled over my outstretched legs. I jumped and made a tiny squeak, mistaking it for a rat. It tumbled to the floor, and fell on its stomach. I saw its eight shiny eyes, looking at me, like a pleading infant. Finding out what it *really* was, I extended my arm, allowing the spider to crawl onto it. After it settled on my forearm, I stroked it gently on its back.

"I'm so sorry, cutie," I apologized quietly to the spider. "I thought you were a nasty rat." I loved spiders. They always seemed friendly to me. Truly, I believed I had a gift for dealing with them. I thought that I was one of the few people who could touch the hearts of these eight-legged arachnids, making them feel comfortable in a human's presence. I don't even know if there *are* any other people like that.

The spider crawled down my wrist. It put a brown, hairy arm on my watch, as if warning me about the time.

My stomach made a somersault, seeing that it was already six-thirty in the evening. I'd been there since breakfast!

I looked around and spotted a wooden set of stairs. Quickly, I patted the spider, thanked it, and set it on the stone-cold floor. *Thanked it*? That was odd.

Not taking much notice on how silly it was to thank the creature, I slowly tiptoed up the creaky wooden steps. Being practical, I peeked through the gap underneath the paint-chipped door. A foot walked by.

Once the footsteps died away, I carefully opened the door. I poked my head out, looking both ways down the long hallway. The coast was clear, so I quietly, but briskly, tiptoed down the hall to the left. On the stony walls, were torches in brackets, and paintings of people who had an unmistakable resemblance to Jenny. The floor was made of fine volcanic glass, which was polished to the extent to which I could see a clear refection of myself.

I made a right turn and went down a corridor. There were more portraits, which were terrifyingly shadowed, due to the firelight of the hallway. A minute later, I came across a life-size portrait of Jenny, who was smiling her proud, non-toothy smile. Gleaming gems bedecked the golden frame. A deep blue one happened to catch my eye. With the tip of my fingers, I gently caressed the eye-catching gem.

To my surprise it glowed. I took a few steps back, a little startled. All of a sudden, the portrait swung back, revealing an opened arching window. I looked at it as if it were pure gold. The window looked right into the woods! I could use it to get home and brew up a plan to help Ryan. What luck!

I started by stretching my left leg out the window, and climbed about a yard down. Before heading home, I placed the portrait in its original position. A girl in her right mind would not do something as foolish as to leave clues. When all was done, I quickly headed towards home.

I went at a swift pace, wanting to get home as soon as possible. In about five minutes, I got to the front door of my cabinlike house. As I reached into my pocket for my key, I felt something smooth and glassy. Quickly, I took it out. It was the bottle of potion, which Ryan was attempting to use on Jenny and her group of girls.

Curiously, I uncorked the tiny bottle. Visible vapors arose, forming the hollow shape of a butterfly. *A butterfly* . . . I thought to myself. "A reverie potion!" I whispered excitedly. I recalled a night when I learned about potions that form shapes made of vapors when opened.

This gave me an idea. I still remembered a thing or two on brewing a reverie potion. It *was* possible to make enough for Jenny and her gang. That would take hours to brew, so I had to start immediately.

I took out my key, and unlocked the door. When I walked in, I found a note tacked to the wall. It had dad's usual at-least-one-mistake on it. I read it.

Allison,
    Your mother and I have gone to the lab for an orientation with a few scientists and the mayor. We'll be back tomorrow afternoon. If you're hungry, dinner's ~~on the stove~~ in the fridge. See you tomorrow.

Love,
Dad

Once I arrived at my room, I grabbed a book on potions, some herbs, spices, a sixteen-ounce glass bottle (which was the shape of an overturned teardrop with a flat tip instead of a pointed one), a funnel, a mini-iron cauldron, and a spell book, just for side reading. After gathering all my needs, I hurried down to the kitchen. It was seven o' clock, and I had no time to lose. I set the cauldron on the stove, turned it on, and poured in a cup and a half of water. Next, I waited till the water started to bubble. When it did so, I opened the book on potions and did the following:

Reverie Potion

1. Add three chopped daisies
2. Drop in half a stick of cinnamon
3. Sprinkle a pinch of sugar
4. Stir for two minutes
5. Put in two halves of mint leaves
6. Pour in a teaspoon of marjoram
7. Beat for another two minutes
8. Let it bubble for three hours, or until butterflies appear

I took a seat at the breakfast table and took out the book of spells. Just for the fun of it, I read the section on death curses and counter-curses. There was one counter-curse I practically memorized.

Three hours later, I peered from the top of the heavy book, and I saw vapor butterflies forming above the steaming cauldron. Quickly, I turned off the heat, and let it cool for a few minutes. Next, I got the bottle and funnel, sticking the funnel in the mouth of the teardroplike bottle. After that, I grabbed the handles of the cauldron and tipped it over the funnel. Once the bottle was filled, I corked it, took it with me, then headed outside. It was eleven o'clock. I had enough time to get to the woods and prepare.

Twenty
The Nightmare

By the time I reached the circular clearing, in which I learned my witchcraft in, it was eleven-twenty. I didn't know what drew me to the coven's rendezvous, but I waited there. My watch ticked away. Eleven thirty . . . eleven forty . . . Suddenly, I heard voices coming from among the trees. Thinking quickly, I hid behind a bush.

". . . Our day has come, girls!" I heard a familiar voice say excitedly.

I peered from the top of the bush, and saw Jenny, walking with the tips of her fingers together. Behind her, was Tay—who was carrying a black sack—and Katrina and Krystine—who were using their telekinesis to keep Ryan in the air. He was tied to the wooden post.

He looked different. On this night, he wasn't wearing his black coat, although I saw him wearing it in the morning, and his hair was flyaway. Instead, he wore a plain white t-shirt. It was odd, seeing him without the coat. It was like his identity, and seeing him without it made him seem like a fraud.

"Within a few hours, our nemesis will be defeated!" Jenny continued. I gasped, forgetting the situation that I was in. Jenny spun around to look towards my direction, frowning slightly.

Luckily, Katrina interrupted her. She panted, "Uh,

Jenny . . . could . . . we . . . let . . . him . . . down? Krystine . . . and . . . I . . . are very . . . very ti . . . tired!"

"Yeah," agreed Krystine, also panting. "We're . . . dying . . . over . . . here!"

"Hmmm?" Jenny glanced at them, and looked back at the bush hiding me. "Oh, yeah. Set him somewhere there," She waved her hand as she carelessly instructed them. She was busy looking at the bush. To my relief, she shrugged and refocused on her evil scheme.

"Now," she started, rubbing her hands together, "any last words?" She strode towards Ryan, ripping off the scotch tape from his lips. *Ooh, that must have hurt!*

"You'll never get away with this!" he gasped.

"Oh, I think I will," she replied, wistfully. "You see, your *friend* is unconscious in my basement. Once we're finished with you," she gave a menacing chuckle, "we will get rid of her! No witness, *no problem!*"

His eyes widened. "You wouldn't dare," he hissed angrily.

"I think I would. Who's going to stop me? *You?*"

For some strange reason, I knew that Ryan and Jenny were having a telepathic conversation. Since I was able to read minds, I decided to eavesdrop.

"*. . . I may be tied to a post, but mind wrestling is a simple task,*" said Ryan.

"*You fool!*" said Jenny. "*Ha! You wouldn't stand a chance!*"

"*Try me!*" He sounded real daring.

Ryan was frowning in anger, and Jenny was smiling a confident smile. I could tell that Ryan was going to make a move. Unfortunately, it looked as if Jenny had already started. His head was thrust back, as if he had been struck on the face. He then looked as if he was being strangled.

"Give it up, *Ryan!*" Jenny taunted. She released him from her mind-grasp. "You and your weakling coven don't stand a *chance* against *my* powerful one!"

"I'd . . . never . . . surrender . . . to . . . you . . . good for nothing . . . **SNOBS!**" he panted. She frowned for a few seconds. She then started to smile a bone-chilling smile. Motioning with her finger from left to right, she calmly replied, "You shouldn't have said that."

From the sack, she took out a tattered spell book. I was guessing that she stole it from Ryan, because it was the same tattered book with a leather binding. Also, she took out a black candle and a match.

After igniting the candle, she turned the old parchment pages, then stopped. She cast another smile at Ryan.

"No!" Ryan whispered, his eyes widened.

I knew now what was happening. My dream—nightmare rather—was coming true. Now, I understood it. It was a warning, or a prophecy. This was terrible. *It's only a nightmare, a big horrible nightmare!* I tried convincing myself. *No. It was not a nightmare. I wasn't going to wake up before the worst this time. What was I to do? Ryan was going to die! I was going to die!*

I stayed glued behind the bush, afraid of being cursed to death.

"Ascendis, ascendis! Bring to me the soul of my utmost enemies!"

"No!"

"May he slash and bleed, that no sore will go nor heed!"

"No!"

"Burn his flesh and eat his voice, may he suffer without any choice!"

"**Nooo!**"

Quickly, before the flash—which was prophesied to strike at any moment—could come, I popped out of the bush. *I'm not going to let that snob kill my friend!* My eyes were fiery with rage. Jenny turned around. *She saw me! She's going to kill me!* The flash appeared. Jenny frowned at me. She was going to mind wrestle me! *I need to do something! I won't let them kill Ryan, never!* Suddenly, before all hope was lost, I had an idea.

"... *How were you planning on getting us to drink this? By throwing it into our mouths?*" I remembered the reverie potion, and Jenny's remark.

I bellowed the words that go along with the potion, "Castiramius Reverio!" I shot some of the potion into Jenny's gaping mouth, by thrusting the bottle, without letting go. By the time she stopped me with her mind, she had already drunk the potion. She collapsed, freeing me from her mental grasp. Without giving it thought, I did the same thing to Krystine, Katrina, and Tay. "Castiramius Reverio!" Within a few seconds, all three of them were on the ground, deep in dream.

The flash was already halfway towards Ryan. My mind began to race. I was yards away from Ryan, and the flash was coming at a fast pace. I ran, ran like I've never ran in my life. When I reached Ryan, the flash was three yards above us. Before I could do something, I screamed, as the flash reached us both.

Although I didn't feel a thing, I continued to scream. It wasn't until a minute later, that I noticed, we weren't going to die. Ryan, who had fainted earlier, opened his eyes, and blinked.

He asked in a pathetic voice, "Are we dead yet?"

"Huh?" I looked up. The flash went up rapidly, then came down, going right through us. "Heh! Whatta ya know? The flash in the sky was merely a harmless hologram."

"*Holo . . . gram?*" he asked weakly. "But how?"

"No time to find out," I said. "We've got to get out of here before *they* wake up." I gestured to the girls on the ground.

I started untying him. Suddenly, something went into my mind. *The bottle of soda!* I knew that Jake wouldn't hurt Ryan, and what would Miss Felton have against him? I thought for a moment, then asked, "Ryan, was that bottle of soda already opened?"

A spider that looked awfully like the one from Jenny's basement scuttled over my shoes and settled in back of me. Its shadow joined mine, which flickered on the trunk of a tree.

"I dunno. I was too thirsty to notice. But I guess it was easier to open than usual."

That's when it hit me. The one behind Ryan's illness on Friday, was a person whom I or anyone else would least suspect. Who else transferred a deadly liquid into a used plastic soda bottle? All along, the culprit was . . .

"Ha, ha, ha, ha!" laughed a cold voice, as the tiny shadow of the spider transformed into that of a human's. "You fools. You blind, *mindless* fools!" I turned around. *It was Howie!*

Twenty-one
The Enemy

"*Howie!*" I hissed.

"Yes. It was *poor, loveless Howie* all along." He blinked. I was a little stunned by what I saw. "What?" he asked, seeing my reaction. "I blinked? Oh, look, I blinked again!" He blinked several times more, being sarcastic. "Well, would you look at that, I'm blinking more!

"Yes, I could blink. I've been able to blink all along. Not blinking and being pathetic, were just sorry excuses for not being a suspect. A *murder* suspect."

My stomach made a horrible jolt. I said in a croak voice, *"Suspect? Murder?"*

He gave me a twisted smile. *"Why of course. You see,"* he lowered his voice, still talking in a cold tone, *"I killed my family."*

"What?" I asked in a shocked whisper. I shook my head in disbelief, "No. No, it was the stick. It was Miss Felton. It had to be—"

"Her?! On the contrary! She *knew* I killed them. She sensed it! In fact, that's why your father got a job here. Since she's the one person here who could see the future, past, and present, she happened to find out my plan for all those people who mocked me, pushed me. The stick thought *you* were the one who could save the town from their doom. What a fool!"

I stood there, dumbfounded for a while. "But how? How did she get my dad a job here? How did she know *me?* What does she see in *me?*"

"Ah, very good questions. Ever since she came to me after finding out what I had done, I've been spying on her. I found out that she told the D.F.S.I.—the Dark Falls Scientific Institute—about your father. They were interested, so they sent him a letter. I, of course, don't know why or how she knew you. Well, whatever. On your way here, you and your parents were put into a trance, allowing you to enter a gateway to this town, without your noticing. All you saw was a pathetic rest stop in a desolate area. That is why you got here quickly."

I stood there for a moment, thinking of something to add to the conversation. I figured that it would spare me some time to think of a plan before he finished us off.

"Er . . . so, then, why *did* you kill your family?" I asked quickly.

"Because I hated them!" he roared, his eyes now shone with fury. "All they wanted was peace for others. They did not want power, but I did. Whenever I tried to increase my powers, they did anything to stop me."

It still didn't make any sense. He killed all his relatives. He was free from their orders and authority. So why did he want to kill Ryan? With this in mind, I asked, not only to spare some time, but out of curiosity, "This doesn't make any sense. What does killing *Ryan* have to do with anything?"

"Oh, he's the main part of it all. And I wouldn't call it *killing.* Consider it as a *sacrifice.* You see, his soul will enhance my powers, and his soul is what I want."

I didn't know what to say. All I did was stare at him in utter disbelief.

"Do you remember that *ring,* Allison? The one you

took your time to find out about in the library? Well, I didn't just find it on the ground and pick it up. I conjured it. When I overheard you at the library as I looked for the book on how to activate the ring, I thought of hiding my plan by saying I *did* find it on the ground. Once I got some power, I took another step higher. I read an entire power enhancement book, until I found the perfect spell. All I needed was the soul of my utmost foe, *and that's you, Ryan.*"

Ryan raised his head in surprise, "Me? But why?"

"You were always my enemy! Ever since that incident! Remember, *buddy?*" *Ryan's* eyes widened, then he lowered his head in shame. "I thought so!" exclaimed Howie.

"What's all this about?" I asked Ryan, in a worried and concerned voice.

Howie answered my question, "One day, Ryan and I were in Salem. A few of the superstitious villagers sensed that we were warlocks. . . ."

As he talked, I saw everything that he said. A mob was chasing nine-year-old Howie and Ryan. They were getting near the face of the cliff, which was the gateway back to Dark Falls. All of a sudden, Howie tripped over a root. He seemed to have fractured one of his wrists.

In a pleading manner, he stuck his uninjured hand out to Ryan and groaned, "Help me, buddy! They're gaining on us!" Cowardly, Ryan ran to the face of the cliff, gave one last terrified glance at him, and disappeared into the rock. The mob crowded Howie and restrained him. Suddenly, I lost the images from my head.

"They took me to a jail house," said Howie. "I managed to escape, however, during the nighttime, vowing to get my revenge!"

I looked at Ryan again. As gently as I could, I asked,

"Is this true?" My voice trembled slightly, hoping that the answer would be no.

To my dismay, he nodded ashamedly, still looking down.

Howie then continued, "I waited a year later. All I needed was more power," he gave a menacing laugh, "so all I needed to do was kill my family. After that, no one would be able to stop me from gaining more power.

"The curse I used was unknown by all, except for the author and me. I found it under a shelf, all dusty and webbed, forsaken by the world. It was called, Ultima Vendicta. Once that was over with, I quit Ryan's coven. If I were to increase my power, I had to be an independent warlock. Besides, I couldn't kill him if I were in his coven. It would be wrong to do so *and* he would have found out anyway.

"After gaining the permission to have more power, then receiving it, I did some research. I still wanted revenge, but I wanted to gain more power as well. With that in mind, I found the perfect spell. It was a power enhancement spell, which required me to kill—*sacrifice*—my foe: The Soul Eater's curse.

"To make it easier to get you into my grasp," he looked at Ryan, "I decided to get you a bit weaker. I got up early Friday morning, brewing a nauseating potion. That was the fluid that blistered your hands." He faced me, a slight grin spreading on his face. "Meant to do that. I'm terribly sorry now."

"That was what Ryan drank," I said in awe, as if I were finally beginning to figure out what the picture of an awkward puzzle was.

"*Yes.* Disguising it as a bottle of soda, and with Jenny also trying to kill him, I got him exactly where I wanted him. All I had to do was convince Stone that I got it from Felton, sweeping off every trace of clues on my path."

He paused, then continued, "Speaking of Jenny, she is how I got you directly into my trap. I knew of the prophecy dream you had, and I decided to imitate it. I transformed into a spider—a new power of mine—and set everything up. I reminded you of the time, got to the wood, and set up the hologram. I knew that Jenny's spell wouldn't work. Her incantation was all wrong. It was totally incomplete! So nothing would have happened if I didn't trigger a false reaction to her spell, and you wouldn't have knocked them out. You know, it's as if you're an accomplice."

"*You wish, you S.O.B!*" I muttered.

He was indifferent. "Do you remember that odd moment in homeroom?" he asked me, his face now inches from mine. I nodded. "Well, that was me. I made sure no one knew that you were tardy." He started to grin. "I froze everybody, which is my unsuccessful work of stopping time. But at least it met with my intentions."

I looked at him, puzzled. Shyly, I asked, "But why did you? How?"

"You could say, I adore your courage and beauty. Ever since I saw you in the woods after the first day of school. When I was passing through the woods, I heard your laughter. From behind the trees I watched you in awe. You were like a sweet, free songbird. Remember? *'Be free, my beautiful songbird. Fly!'* " He sighed. "I'd use all my powers to help you any day."

I continued to look at him in utter confusion and sickness. *This psycho had a crush on me!* I then asked slowly, "That time Mister Cross excused me from detention, was that because of you?"

"Why, yes. When I got his attention, I scrambled up

his brain a bit, making him do what I command him to do telepathically. That of course, explains that dinosaur remark. I was just having fun with him."

Howie smiled at me broadly yet in a twisted way for a moment, then his face darkened. "But enough about that!" Vines rose from nowhere, as he raised his own hands. I was suddenly tied tightly with them. He had both a look of fury and somehow, of bitter joy. "I think you're cute, but I, like Jenny, cannot have a witness lying around. Say your prayers, you two, it's time to die!"

"No!" I pleaded dryly, as Ryan and I struggled vainly in our restraints.

"Adios!" He pried out the black candle from Jenny's hand, took a lighter from his pants pocket, and lit the candle. He took a tiny bottle from the same pocket. As he shook the bottle at our feet, ash came pouring out. He took out a black candleholder the shape of a scull, placed the candle in it, and set it on the ground between Ryan and me.

Suddenly, he rolled his eyes back, showing only milky white balls in his sockets. He then started talking in a haunting voice that sounded to me like the devil himself. It sounded as if he were possessed by some exorcist.

"Soul Eaters, Soul Eaters, I command you, in the name of Lucifer, to unleash the demons of hell! May they take the enemy of the wicked to the realm of the dead, where the lake of fire and brimstone gorges on your flesh, and the souls weep in agony!"

Halfway through the spell, I got an idea. The counter-curse, what was it? If I used it, I would kill Howie. His spell wouldn't work if I stopped him from completing the spell. *If only I could remember . . .*

"Ascendis, ascendis! Bring to me the soul of my utmost enemies!" he went on as I frantically struggled to remember. "May he slash and bleed, that no sore will go nor heed!"

Suddenly, like a lighter that somebody tried to light finally flickering, the thought struck me. In an overpowering voice, I said, "Bring peace to the innocent, and cast away the wicked! Bring us peace! Bring us peace!"

Howie stopped once he heard me. He knew what I was doing. In the same deep devilish way, his eyes still rolled back, he yelled, "What are you doing? Stop that!"

As he staggered towards me, I quickly continued, "Cast his soul to the land of the dead, and may he be locked away in eternal darkness! Cast his soul! Cast his soul!"

Suddenly, he yelled, "**Nooo!!!**" At that moment, at least fifty translucent figures in translucent hooded cloaks shot out from the treetops. Their faces were like those of skulls with razor-sharp teeth. They all circulated around Howie in such a speed that they looked like a giant white hula-hoop. I heard Howie yell once more, then, there was a powerful light from the center of the ring, beaming heavenwards, followed by a powerful explosion.

This resulted in a powerful gust of wind. Since Ryan and I were bound to the ground, we stayed put, but Jenny, Tay, Krystine, and Katrina, who were lying on the ground, were swept into the trees. Within minutes, the deafening sound of the explosion ceased echoing, and all was calm.

The sun began to rise above us, presenting a new day. Howie's power was no longer there to control the vines that bound me, so as I stretched my aching wrists, I found that they were free, and so was the rest of me. I looked around. Howie was lying dead on the ground. Next to me was Ryan, who was still bound up and he had fainted once more. Through the trees, I saw Jenny, Katrina, Krystine, and Tay get up and emerge from the trees.

"What the heck happened?" asked Jenny in shock. She walked over to Ryan and plucked out a few hairs from his head.

"Ow!" he exclaimed, waking up.

"Why isn't he dead?!"

I looked at her, and though I'd just been through the worst, smiled. "I'll tell you everything on the way home."

"Well, all right." She sounded tired, but instead of being cranky and impatient, she cooperated.

After Ryan was untied, we walked Jenny home. Howie rode on Ryan's back. I told them everything, from the escape from Jenny's basement, to the part when everyone had awoken.

"So, Blanks is *dead?*" asked Jenny, after hearing all I had to say. " 'Cause of *you?*"

"Yeah."

"I can't believe it! That *twerp* actually tried to kill you, *Ryanna!*"

"Yeah, yeah," muttered Ryan.

"I still can't get over this," said Jenny, putting her hand over her forehead. "I need some sleep." We had already arrived at Jenny's mansion. She muttered something, and the gates slid open. She went through, the other three following.

"Bye!" I called out to them, trying to be friendly.

"Yeah, whatever."

Ryan and I headed to his house. On the way, we came across Miss Felton, who was strolling through the wood. She looked at us broadly, looking very cheerful.

"Oh, hello, Miss Felton!" I greeted, trying to sound as bright as her face.

"Why, hello, you two!" she said in return. Her voice

was full of joy. "Well, good day to you both!" She glanced at Howie's dead body. "Need any help?" She sounded a bit more serious.

"Ye—" Ryan tried to say, but I interrupted him.

"No! No, thank you. We're fine."

"Well, okay." She bent down and said into my ear, "Excellent job! You've saved us all!"

I looked up to see that she had vanished.

"She knew about what happened?" I asked quietly.

"I guess. Listen, we've got to get to my house. I can't just keep him on my back all day!"

"Oh! I'm sorry. I forgot!"

Twenty-two
A Day to Remember

We arrived at Ryan's house a few minutes later. I was stunned by the sight of his home. Behind a gate similar to Jenny's was a marble-tiled path leading to a giant white mansion, with four marble pillars standing at the front. It was an ancient Greek-styled house.

I studied the frieze. It bore the image of a girl standing in front of a crowd. She seemed to be leading them somewhere. Apparently, she was Tuyen Lee, leading the witches and warlocks to Dark Falls.

"You have a *lovely* abode!" I commented to Ryan in awe.

"Yeah, it's great," he mumbled.

He led me to the door. A man in a black suit and a red bow tie stood at the door. "Good morning, Young Master Nakano," he greeted with a British accent. The man opened the door with a white-gloved hand.

"Yeah, yeah, Montgomery," mumbled Ryan in return, as he slouched into the entrance hall. Montgomery grimaced as Howie's corpse passed his nostrils.

The large entrance hall was decorated with suits of armor and gold-framed paintings. Before us, was another door, this time guarded by a fairly full-figured woman. She greeted politely. "Why good morning, Young Master Nakano." No one seemed to take much notice of the corpse on Ryan's back, me, or the fact that he was out during the night. We both entered through the door as Ryan again mumbled.

We entered a room that was probably as large as my house, and the ceiling—which had gleaming crystal chandeliers hanging from it—was probably higher than my house. There were three circles of wine-red velvet, antique couches and glass coffee tables, a few side tables, and more paintings. At the far end of the room were two sets of stairs on either side of a balcony. Unlike most balconies, the platform faced inward. There, I saw a man, who was wearing an elegant black tuxedo, playing Ludwig van Beethoven's *Für Elise,* on a black grand piano. Next to him was a beautiful woman, dressed in an elaborate, blood-red, satin gown, which was sleeveless.

"Hi, Mom! Hi, Dad," Ryan called out, sounding worn out.

The man stopped playing, and the two of them looked down. "Oh, hello, son!" shouted the man grandly. "Where have you been?"

"I'll explain later, sir."

"Who are your friends? Are you going to introduce them as a *proper* young man like yourself should?"

"Not *friends,* Mom." I looked down, put down by his reply. He then finished a few seconds later, "Only *she's* my friend." He tapped my shoulder.

"Oh, how lovely! But then, whoever is that on your back?"

"Howie Blanks, ma'am."

"*Howie Blanks?* I thought he *was* your friend."

"*Friends don't try to kill you,*" he muttered.

"What was that?"

"Huh? Nothing. Um, please sit for a moment. I'd like

to explain to you why I was gone." He patted one of the couches.

"Well, all right."

The two of them stepped down to meet me. "Hello," greeted the woman, giving me a firm handshake. "I'm Mayor Alicia Nakano, Ryan's mother, and this is my husband, Eleazar."

"Hello," I replied politely. I was a little startled to hear that I was being greeted by the mayor. "I'm Allison. Allison Romero. It's such a pleasure to meet you both."

"*Romero,* did you say?"

"Yes. Yes I did."

"You must be the daughter of April and Jay-Ar Romero then, are you not?"

"Yes, I am."

"Well, now! They must have told you they'd be with me, right?" I nodded. "Well, I'm sorry to say that I had to leave a tad bit early. It was hard leaving them. They are such interesting people."

I smiled.

Ryan laid Howie on a couch in another circle. Mister and Mayor Nakano looked at the corpse. "Asleep?" asked Mister Nakano.

My stomach lurched when he asked that. Ryan and I exchanged nervous glances. He replied worriedly, "Um, that'll be explained as I explain my being out."

Soon, we were all gathered around a coffee table, listening to Ryan relive our horrifying experience. He went from detail to horrifying detail. I felt the horror rush back into me.

Ryan finished, and Mrs. Nakano had a worried face. You might think that it was because of her son's horrible experience, or that his former coven member was the one behind the *Heinous Curse of '98,* but that wasn't the reason for her worried expression. She asked with disgust, "So, the boy lying on one of our fine antique couches *is dead?*"

"Yes," replied Ryan, sounding a little disappointed when hearing that his mother showed more concern for a piece of furniture than for him.

She paled. With a worried, disgusted smile, she nodded. She took a cell phone from her purse, which was on the coffee table, and dialed a number. "Hello? Montgomery? Yes. Could you call the furniture shop? Which one? The antique one. The one near that clock shop, *Time Flies.* Tell them to take away an unwanted couch of mine." She glanced at the pale corpse. She added, "And call the morgue. Tell them we have a corpse."

We were somewhere just outside the woods, past the artificial waterfall. It was a place I had never been before. There were founts of water pouring down from the top of flowery hills, which surrounded the grassy land, where there were few trees, that were covered with violate blossoms. The blossoms gently sprinkled on the crowd of people, as did the colorful leaves in the woods. The only thing that darkened this place was the fact that it was a cemetery.

It was rather clean and well maintained. There were no tombstones, just marble plaques, stuck to the ground, which labeled information of the people who lay six feet under. The mayor was at the front of the crowed, beside Howie's coffin, and in front of the hole in which it was to be buried. She was talking about Howie's death, and the cause of it. I was up next, to tell them in detail, exactly what happened, and why I had to send this teenage boy to an early grave, no matter how heartbreaking it was for me to talk about it.

I faced the crowd made up of Howie's foster parents, their relatives, Ryan, his parents, reporters, and news cameras. "Hello, honorary guests, people of Dark Falls." I started to get a little teary. "Just a few horrifying hours ago, Howie Blanks attempted murder with witchcraft on Ryan Nakano, our mayor's son, and me. He also confessed things to us that were unimaginable . . ." I continued talking, though my heart started filling up with terror and despair.

As I talked, I looked at each person's face, and I spotted Karen and Phanny. I guessed that they saw the crowd when they had come back from Salem. They watched me in horror and in surprise, as I talked on about what had happened when they were away. Every time I stopped talking, I'd see on their faces smiles of encouragement. Friendship. It's what gave me the courage to finish my story.

". . . And though Howie nearly killed us, I do feel, that even *I* should have respect for his death. I wish there was some other way to have stopped this madness, in any other way but to have killed him, but there was no other choice. Talking it over wasn't going to stop him from doing his greedy curse." I hung my head low for a moment, then looked up again. "That's—that's pretty much all I could say. Thank you."

There was silence for a moment. The mayor then asked for any final good-byes. There were none. Soon, the funeral was over. Howie was six feet under the ground, and we had nothing to worry about.

Although it was Monday, there was no school. This day of June 11, 2001 was the day celebrating my saving the town. There was a quick ceremony after the funeral. I received a gold medal, and the day was declared as a local holiday.

It was such an honor. It was too bad that my parents didn't know about it. *My parents!* That's what came into my mind while Karen, Phanny, and Ryan came up to congratulate me.

"Wow!" exclaimed Phanny. "You've practically saved our lives, and you're not even a witch yet!" exclaimed Phanny. "And to think, we missed it all!"

For the first time, Karen took notice in my work. "Yeah," she agreed in a tone of surprise. "That was very brave of you." She looked down for a moment, then said, "Thanks. Thanks a lot."

"Hey," said Ryan, as he walked over and joined us, "I'd really like to thank you for what you did. You were brave, saving me with magic. I would be dead, and this whole town would be doomed if it weren't for you."

I blushed. "It was nothing," I muttered.

"But *why?*" started Ryan slowly. "Why did you take all those chances, those risks, only to save *me,* Ryan the *Loser?*"

"Because you're my *friend!* Being there for the other! Sacrificing one's self for the one in peril!" I paused, and let a tear of warm, sentimental feeling roll silently down my cheek. I then added, "You all are my friends. I'd go through this whole trauma over again than lose any of you!"

There was a short silence. All of a sudden, Phanny broke the ice. "That was so beautiful!" she cried, giving me a teddy bear hug.

The other two skeptically drew nearer to the sobbing Phanny. Suddenly, she swooped them up too—Okay, cut that out! It just gets a little *too mushy there! Ugh! The people reading this will think that we're mental or some-*

thing, hugging each other like mad! Skip that part. Okay, go on!

My parents, I thought again. "Oh, yeah. Phanny," I said quickly, "do you want to see my dad's lab?"

"*Lab?* What lab?" She looked really confused.

"*Remember?* The one he was talking about during lunch on Saturday?"

"Oh, yeah," she answered, still very clue-less.

"Gee, the last time you heard about it, you couldn't keep your mind off seeing it."

Something came across my mind once more. I forgot to tell them about my nightmare. It was a prophecy, a warning. Well, it was too late to tell them, but I still wanted to inform them anyway. "You know, there was something I meant to tell you. I kind of, I don't know, had a feeling about the thing that happened a few hours ago."

"What do you mean?" asked Karen.

"Well, you see, the night before we moved here, I had a nightmare. It was about Ryan and Jenny. Jenny was about to curse Ryan, who was on a post. It happened in a jumbled package."

"What do you mean by *that?*"

"The things that happened—except for the part with Howie—happened. It all just happened out of order. Like the flash. It appeared *right after* I bellowed *castiramius reverio* in the dream."

"*Wow*," said Phanny in wonder. "It's like a prophecy or déjà vu!"

"I know."

"That's not a really common dream," remarked Ryan, looking as though he were trying to solve a long and complicated algebraic equation.

"No, of course not," said the tough voice of a British

woman. We turned around and saw Miss Felton standing tall, broadly smiling down at us.

"Oh, Miss Felton!" I said in surprise. "Hello!"

"Hello, young lady. I just wanted to drop by and congratulate you. Thanks to you, we're all safe."

"Miss," said Phanny, wistfully, "do you know anything about this?"

I looked at the P.E. teacher and remembered what Howie had told me about her.

She smiled, "Why, of course. I was the one who sent for her. I needed a reason for having her here before Howie's final destructiveness began to arise. I got her parents a job here to do so. Her father received a letter that told him that he got a promotion, and it contained directions to Dark Falls.

"The directions indicated that Dark Falls was northeast of Los Angeles. They took the route, and just before entering the Mojave Desert, the three of you were put into a trance, as you entered a secret gateway that brought you all the way across the country in the period of two hours."

"I'm sorry to interrupt," I interrupted, "but I was just wondering, how were we put into a trance?"

"Ah, good question. You see, you might already know that Dark Falls is a whole different world, and magic here, is more than spells, curses, and incantations. Here, some people have the ability to do divination, to enchant things, and even to fly.

"I for one, can actually enchant or entrance people at far distances, and see the past, present, and future. I could look into a cauldron of boiling reverie potion, visualize you near the gateway, and entrance you on the spot. And that is what I did."

"Wow," I said in awe. "That's incredible!"

"Yes, but quite difficult."

I thought for a moment. This still did not explain my nightmare, nor did it my being chosen to save Dark Falls from a destructive end. I guessed that Miss Felton had noticed this, because in a few minutes, that's what she started to clear up.

"That dream," she began, "was brought to you by me. I did the same thing I did to entrance you, but a tad bit differently. Instead of visualizing your route, I went into your mind. I saw what would come in the future, and I tried to plant that into your head as if it were a dream. It was a little mixed up when I transferred the information, but I thought you'd have an idea.

"I had chosen you, someone who has not been associated with witchcraft before, because you seemed more determined, brave, and loyal to friends than anyone else. I saw all that in you. When I saw you in the woods with Ryan, I excitedly told the principal, Mister Khealer about your arrival. Since you and Ryan were already acquainted, I told him to send your program slip to him. It included your address."

"How did you even see me? How did you know me?"

"That, I don't know. You just happened to appear in one of my visions. You were defending a younger boy then. I was interested, so I continued to watch you."

"I remember that," I said, thoughtfully. "I was walking through the lunch area at the beginning of seventh grade, which was at my previous school, and saw a mean, large eighth grader picking on a sixth grader. I just can't stand seeing people being bullied. So I went up to him and firmly spoke up. He had the boy's backpack, so I told him to give the backpack back or he'd deal with me. I don't know why he gave the backpack instantly at those words, because I was much shorter than him, and weaker."

Miss Felton smiled again. "You probably already had magic in you—dark magic."

"But she's full of virtue," said Ryan, confused. "Why would she have darkness in her?"

"*Mmmm, I don't know.* She did kill that evil boy with a very powerful counter-curse, didn't she?"

"Well, I guess your—" He stopped. Once again, Miss Felton had vanished.

"She's gone," I whispered.

"Bah! I could do that too!" said Phanny.

"So could Ryan and I," Karen added.

As we walked, I hardly noticed that we weren't heading towards my house. Instead, Ryan led us to the school.

"What are we doing here?" I asked, finally realizing where we were.

Ryan smiled excitedly, leading us to the back of the school. We were in front of double doors that had a gold Chinese dragon with jade eyes over it. "Remember all those times I've disappeared at school?"

My eyes widened. "Oh, yeah! Are you going to tell me why now?" I asked excitedly.

"I could *tell* you, but I'd rather *show* you. Welcome to the school's never-will-be-used-again auditorium."

He pushed open the auditorium doors.

There was a sudden "Surprise!" as hundreds of people popped from behind tables of wrapped presents and refreshments. I was taken aback. The entire school—including the faculty and administrators—were among the people. I looked up, and saw a festive banner saying: *Happy Late Birthday Allison Romero!!!* There was a band on the stage, playing tasteful pop music. Tacked to the stage, was a banner saying, *"Playing live: The Warwick Warlocks."*

"You've thrown me a birthday party?" I looked at Ryan.

"Yup! Ever since I found out the date on your program slip, I decided to do this. I did the planning, decorating, and inviting each time I left your side at school. I even had to do research on Cheering Potions. You know, to get them to be cheery. After that, I had to test them on myself. Once that was done, I had to inject it into every single student in school; no easier way, eh!" he added with an *I'm-so-clever smile*. "Sorry it's late, though, and, sorry we couldn't get the Back Street Boys. But the Warwick Warlocks are the closest to the Back Street Boys as we can get."

I grinned from ear to ear. "What do you mean, *sorry?* You barely knew me and already gave thought to my birthday! No one's ever cared for my birthday!" I flung my arms around Ryan, Karen, and Phanny, not mentioning that sneaking the potion into snacks and offering them would probably have been more simple.

I let go. "Besides," I said, "I should be saying sorry to *you, Ryan!* I was the one who broke your leg at homeroom, I was angry, and I—"

"Oh, who cares!" said Ryan, ushering me through the crowd. "Just mingle a little. It's your party! You deserve some fun, *friend.*" He disappeared into the crowd. I turned around. *The guy purposely put me next to Jake Stone!*

"Uh, hi!" I said, blushing.

"Hey, Allison! Great party! Wanna dance!" He was smiling with joy, flashing pearly white teeth.

"Er, sure, I guess," I said with a smile, moving with the music.

It was wonderful! I saved the whole of Dark Falls, saved a friend, a holiday was made in honor of me, and I was at *my* birthday bash, dancing to tasteful music with Jake Stone. Now, when I think of my "cursed" birthday, I think of how great life was turning out, and I probably wasn't cursed after all. Dark Falls was where I planned to live forever as a famous witch, the happiest one ever!

AND SO ON...

The following Friday night, I became a member of the coven. I did not need to take the witchcraft test, because I had proved myself to be witch-worthy. Not only was I accepted into the coven, but Ryan chose me as the new leader. Being the leader of the coven, I decided to change its name. It then became: The Lucky Coven (TLC). Truly, we were lucky. (I actually mean that *I'm* lucky.) I only knew that counter curse because, out of sheer luck, I just happened to come across the counter curse, and I just *happened* to memorize it, that's all. What, do you think that I was destined to save Dark Falls because I was some blessed witch with a Friday the Thirteenth birthday and a serpent birthmark? No, no, you've been *way* over you're head on this!

Well, if you don't think that's considered lucky, well then, let me tell you this: having three of the most amazing friends in the world is what I consider to be the luckiest thing of all!

Karen trusted me more, knowing that I could handle witchcraft just as well. She would always ask me how I defeated Howie. I would always say that I didn't have a clue. It was true, I didn't. The whole thing just seemed to have happened.

My life has been going well so far. I actually became very popular. *Me, Allison Romero.* Truly, it was quite a miracle! I'm in a lot of books such as *The Darkness Defeated; What Happened on June 11th?; The Mystery of the Normal Girl;* and even *The Little Girl That Could*—though it looked like someone taped the word

"Girl" over the word "Engine." Everyone at school asks me to relive the tragedy that made the biggest climax in my entire life. It's very hard, but I usually do so.

And to think I'm trying to hide all that from my parents! They still don't know about me, the other inhabitants, the fast growing media on the me-defeating-Howie thing, or that this holiday that was in honor of my victory—which is, by the way, called the Day of the New Light. I know that next year, they'll find out about the holiday, but I'll make sure that they never find out about its purpose, at least, until I'm ready to give them the unbelievable, thunder-striking information that I was given to on my first day at Dark Falls Junior High. Hey, look's like I've got a book to write, eh?

Because I came to attend school there in May, which is a month before summer vacation, I only went to school for two weeks more after my grand victory. On June 22, the eighth graders left, and the school year was over till September. I decided to spend a lot more time in the woods during the summer, and get to get stronger with witchcraft. I even started to learn to speak and read Egyptian. In fact, everyone kept saying "RA!" in the streets on the day of my victory. "RA" means sun, I think. It fits. Ra, sun, light, my victory . . . okay, I should go now!

Well, that's all. Good-bye for now! Oh, and by the way, Dad's lab, it's the bomb!

**—This story was based on a weird
 witchy girl whom
 you couldn't possibly know.**